Batik

Batik

with NOEL DYRENFORTH

JOHN HOUSTON

BOBBS-MERRILL
INDIANAPOLIS · NEW YORK

Q
746.6
D 994b

The publishers wish to acknowledge the help of the
following artists: Dr Amri Yahya, Thetis Blacker, Juliet
Bloye, Charlotte Freeman, Deryck Henley, Sylvia Nestor
Robinson, Michael O'Connell and Norma Starszakowna
who have contributed their work to this book. They also
wish to acknowledge the help of the Indonesian
Women's Association, London.
Studio photography by John Price.
Other photographs were supplied by the following:
Page 12: Douglas Dickins; pages 13 and 17: L. H.
Hoddenbagh, Museum voor land en Volkenkunde,
Rotterdam; page 15: Picturepoint; page 25: I.G.D.A.;
page 68, centre: Charlotte Freeman; page 70: Sylvia
Nestor Robinson; page 71, top left: Deryck Henley;
page 72: Rudolf Smend.

Published by The Bobbs-Merrill Company, Inc.
Indianapolis/New York
ISBN 0-672-52179-2
Library of Congress Catalog Card Number: 75-13836
Manufactured in Italy by IGDA, Novara
First U.S. printing

CONTENTS

WORKING WITH BATIK

I first started working with batik by simply toying with the various tools and materials, exploring the potential of the craft. I soon discovered that the molten wax had a particular character of its own and that dyeing fabric is not just putting colour on a surface in the way a painter might, but rather a matter of colour penetrating the structure of a fabric. In my first experiments, the way in which colour and form interacted through the sequence of waxings and dyeings seemed almost magical. Gradually, however, I found that I could strike a balance between the nature of the medium and my objectives as an artist. This changing balance between technique and design is the source of very creative and exciting effects. The finished batik is often the result of countless readjustments. I have always tried to avoid rigid methods and recipes, often benefiting from taking risks and sometimes using accidents to open up new approaches.

Besides its obvious role as a decorative craft, batik can convey a personal statement. I hope that this book will bring more people into contact with the craft, and that they will be able to share my enjoyment of this vital and rewarding medium.

Noel Dyrenforth

FABRIC, WAX AND DYE

The essentials of the craft • its creative possibilities • how to use this book

Batik, simply, is fabric, wax, and dye. Shapes, patterns, and lines are drawn directly onto the fabric with molten wax. When the fabric is dyed, these waxed areas resist the dye-colour thus preserving the fabric's original colour as a negative image. New waxings and fresh applications of different dyes can elaborate the pattern and enrich the range of colour. Finally, the layers of wax are removed when the design is complete.

Batik is the most subtle and expressive of the resist methods as the ready flow of molten wax encourages painter-like and graphic techniques. The techniques of batik allow even the most personal experiments to merge gracefully with many different design traditions. This harmonious blending of styles is demonstrated in this book by the work of Noel Dyrenforth, one of the world's leading batik artists.

He has adapted the range of traditional Oriental techniques to contemporary methods and materials. His international reputation is based on batiks which rival paintings in their expressive qualities, but still retain the rich transparencies and textures of a dyed fabric. His work appears in many private collections as well as in Britain's major public collection of decorative art, the Victoria and Albert Museum.

In the Orient, batik has never been categorized simply as an art form. It is considered far more as a practical skill than as a decorative art. Noel Dyrenforth maintains this wider view by extending batik to dress

Left: This Indonesian girl wears a traditional batik cloth as a sarong. The same cloth can be worn in several ways: as a cloth wrapped around the bust, folded into a broad waistband or tied into a sling across one shoulder to carry a baby or a bundle. This design centres on a motif of eagle's wings, the most ancient of the Javanese patterns. The cotton cloth is a *tulis* batik, one worked entirely with a tjanting, the traditional implement for drawing with wax. The design on the fan shows characters from the *Wayang Kulit*, the silhouette puppets of Java. These were the only human forms which Muslim artists were allowed to depict

design and to soft sculpture. In later sections of this book we demonstrate these techniques and suggest other uses for batik.

Hardly any special equipment is needed to do batik. Most households will already have an iron, rubber gloves and a suitable plastic, stainless steel, or enamel vessel — although these are luxuries which batik craftsmen have had to do without for hundreds of years!

The skills and examples we will examine have been chosen from the wide range of traditions developed through the centuries in India, Japan, China, and Java. Most experts consider Javanese batik to be the classic form — even the word 'batik' is Javanese. The Javanese batik has developed an unequalled delicacy and precision, massing finely detailed silhouettes of birds, flowers and animals into densely packed geometric frames. These fabrics were all made to be worn as square or rectangular cloths, folded and draped around the waist, shoulder or head. In Western collections, however, they are usually displayed as wall-hangings which emphasize the crisp patterns and maze-like rhythms normally concealed when worn. It also exposes the craftsman's virtuoso use of the tjanting, a drawing instrument with a cup and spout from which molten wax is poured. The tjanting allows the flow of liquid wax to be controlled as delicately as the user's own handwriting, and encourages the same kind of personal expression. Noel Dyrenforth uses it extensively in his work, where the tjanting's flickering line is offset by the ample forms and sonorous colours that are the basis of his individual style.

The most characteristic feature of batik is the crackle, the delicate network of hair-thin lines which develop throughout the design when dye is allowed to seep into cracks in the waxed areas. This effect has the seductive charm of a happy accident, yet it is possible to control and vary this subtle veining by the use of special wax or by applying dye with a brush rather than immersing the fabric in the dye. Many fine batiks make little use of crackle, however, just as many artists have produced complex work without relying on the tjanting. Any instrument that carries molten wax safely from the heated pot to the fabric is usable: spoons, old paint brushes, perforated cans that drip and trail the wax. Most craftsmen devise their own range of tools in mastering the technique, and they often end by discarding all but one or two known and tried favourites.

This book proceeds by example, and while the demonstrations are intended to show how it is done, they also stand as evidence of a master craftsman's experience. Noel Dyrenforth's recipes for dyes, waxes and colour combinations given at the end of this book will prove invaluable in mastering the early stages of batik. We close with an international listing of craft societies to enable readers to make contact with others interested in the art of batik — to exchange designs, techniques, dye recipes and to keep in touch with the major craftsmen in the field.

Right: *Life Centre* is the most symmetrical of Noel Dyrenforth's batiks. The dark central disc is patterned with tjanting-drawn dots and jagged lines. All the other softer, brighter forms cluster around this circle with tjanting calligraphy added after the first dyeing. Procion M fibre-reactive dyes were used, first in pink, followed by orange, then red, and finally the darkest dye, a mixture of three parts navy blue to one part brown. The rich background shows the effect of adding all four dyes

TRADITION AND THE CRAFT

How and where batik developed • the traditional tools and techniques of the Far East • batik comes to the West

The Javanese word *batik* is relatively modern, first appearing in Dutch texts in the early seventeenth century. It derives from *ambatik* which refers to the whole range of activities of drawing, painting, tattooing and writing. A much older term, *tulis*, meaning handwriting, still survives but now refers exclusively to the dwindling number of batiks which are painted entirely by hand.

Batik evolved several traditions of design and technique which blended together over the centuries through different cultures. Indian cotton, Chinese silk, Buddhist, Mohammedan, and Hindu imagery, were all mixed into the traditions of the craft and produced, particularly in Java, an art of courtly elegance that retained its delicacy even at the level of village industry.

Batik uses the same principle as all the resist methods. These methods create a barrier between areas of the fabric and the action of a dye. The tie-dye method is probably the simplest example of this principle and possibly the earliest resist method used. A piece of material pleated lengthwise and then tied tightly with string will resist the action of dye inside those bound sections. When untied, the fabric will be patterned with regular stripes in its original colour, alternating with bands of the dye-colour. Even this, the most basic of all the resist methods, can produce varied effects of great subtlety. A characteristic feature of tie-dye is the delicate gradations of dye colour at the edges of resist areas.

Other basic resist methods are used to produce similar types of pattern. *Kyokechi* was a Japanese method of dyeing fabric by jamming it between patterned boards. The fabric was stretched taut across a wooden block on which the pattern was carved in relief. A second block, with an exact mirror image of the pattern, was pressed against the other side of the fabric, with the two images precisely matched. The two blocks were bound together, exerting maximum pressure on the fabric, and this

Right: The geometric pattern of triangles with their points opposed identifies this pattern as part of a sarong. This always forms the centre panel of skirt cloths and is known as the head, or *kapala*. This section of the design is of medieval origin and illustrates the rigidly conservative character of traditional Javanese design

Below: An Indonesian craftswoman uses the tjanting to draw the first wax outlines of a traditional design. The fabric is not stretched but simply hung over a rail

Above: Indonesian craftsman using the technique of printing with molten wax. The complicated motifs of hand-drawn patterns are copied with great skill by the block-makers, who fix narrow bands of copper sheet, edge up, into a piece of wood. These blocks, or *tjaps*, are made in pairs, each a perfect mirror image of the other. They can then be used to print on both sides of the fabric simultaneously, thus making sure that the wax penetrates perfectly

sandwich was then lowered into the dye bath. Pressure prevented dye from reaching the patterned area, and an image was created in negative. Most Japanese and many Chinese resist methods aimed at this kind of precise, repeatable impression. Many of the fabrics are decorated with stencils so complicated and delicate that the many parts were joined by single strands of human hair.

Unlike the closed societies of China and Japan, where the character of design depended simply on the fashions set by the Imperial Courts, Java was continually subjected to foreign influences. The Kingdom of Java, however, which extended roughly over the same territory as modern Indonesia, still preserved a cultural unity. This unity is reflected in the unique character of Javanese batik which absorbed and blended many influences into its own traditions. The Hindu religion which came to Java from India kept open a route through which the growing power of Islam spread to dominate Java. This is clearly reflected in the character of the designs. In batik the densely packed texture of Hindu decoration was slowly rearranged to accept Muslim motifs, but the density of the pattern remained peculiarly Javanese. Although Muslim rule prohibits the representation of the human figure, this seems to have had little effect on Javanese design which has always maintained the pre-Islamic tradition.

Batik is practised in Java as a normal, year round outdoor activity. Traditionally men prepared the fabric while women waxed the designs. These craftsmen and women ranked well above the peasants who could only afford to barter for the most crudely decorated cloths, mass produced with a simple multiple technique. This technique consisted of several layers of cloth arranged to absorb a single application of wax. The bottom cloth, which would have a vague and blurred design, was the cheapest. Another economy was the refurbishing of old, faded batiks. This involved the use of a rice-paste resist to

Below: Women and girls in a Javanese workshop feed the cloth across their knee as they work methodically from one end to the other with the tjanting. Although each woman faces a different direction, working positions are set so that a centrally placed wax pot can be shared by several women. The largest cloths measure 7 feet by 11½ feet (2·1 m by 3·5 m) and the waxings required can take one woman two weeks to complete. The number of these *tulis* batiks is steadily declining and tjap and tjanting techniques are usually combined

redefine the design before redyeing. But this required boiling in order to remove the resist, and old cloths seldom survived the treatment. Cheapest of all was a stencil technique, using lacquered paper and a soya bean paste resist that could be scraped and rubbed off the dyed cloth.

True Javanese batik was a laborious and costly process. Elaborate preparations made the fabric supple and sensitive so that wax and dye would achieve the maximum effect. A single waxing — some thousands of lines and dots drawn with the tjanting — could take several days. After each dyeing all wax was removed, and the process repeated: preparation, second waxing, second dyeing, wax removed, and so on through several dyeings. This complete re-waxing at each stage accounts for the sharpness of each detail. The complete removal of wax after each dyeing avoided the building up of wax layers which could produce the crackle effect. Crackle, which is often regarded as batik's most attractive characteristic in the West, is seen as evidence of poor craftsmanship in many areas of Java.

The origin of the tjanting is of crucial importance in the development of batik. This pen-like instrument was, and is, the mainstay of Javanese batik as we now know it. Everywhere else in the world, liquid resist was traditionally applied with much more primitive instruments. In India the hot wax flowed from a wadded bundle of hemp or rags wrapped around a metal stem with a painted tip which acted as a kind of crude nib. Bamboo quills, or sharpened sticks with wax or rice-paste were used in China and Japan. But the tjanting is a more sophisticated instrument than any of these. An open reservoir holds a supply of hot wax which flows onto the fabric through a narrow, curved spout. Reservoir and spout are a single unit, formed from thin copper sheet, and set on a straight bamboo handle. Each tjanting is specially built to make a certain type of mark; some have five or six nozzles arranged in a row to draw a series of parallel lines. The earliest Javanese batiks used sticks and brushes to apply a starch-paste resist to a coarse cotton cloth but these were crude, one colour batiks. It has been suggested that the tjanting technique was first used at the Javanese Royal Courts, in the same way that embroidery was used at the European Courts, and that this instrument was developed as an efficient, clean and therefore dignified applicator for wax.

In 1835 Dutch firms began to imitate batiks and tried to sell them in Java. The possibility of selling European goods within a colonial empire stood trade on its head! This curious trade grew quickly in the later part of the century as Britain allowed free trade with India and Swiss firms joined the Dutch in mass producing batiks. In England and Switzerland huge roller presses printed batik designs complete with fake irregularities and imitation veining. The machines were even treated with patchouli oil to make these 'batiks' smell authentic. In Holland wooden blocks produced a close imitation of a new technique introduced to Java in the mid-nineteenth century. This method used the *tjap*, a block set with a raised copper pattern used to print the wax resist on the front and back of fabrics. This new method could wax 250 sarongs in the time taken to draw the same pattern on one cloth with the tjanting.

This extraordinary trade petered out at the beginning of the First World War, but by that time some European firms had achieved almost perfect imitations of true batik. The revival of interest in the arts and crafts in Western Europe in the late nineteenth century made real batik a technique favoured by amateur and professional artists in Holland, Germany, and Austria. Since then international fashion has exploited either the technique or its design tradition at various times. A growing number of artists and craftsmen throughout the world are responding more seriously to batik as the most distinctive and expressive of all the resist techniques and an art in its own right.

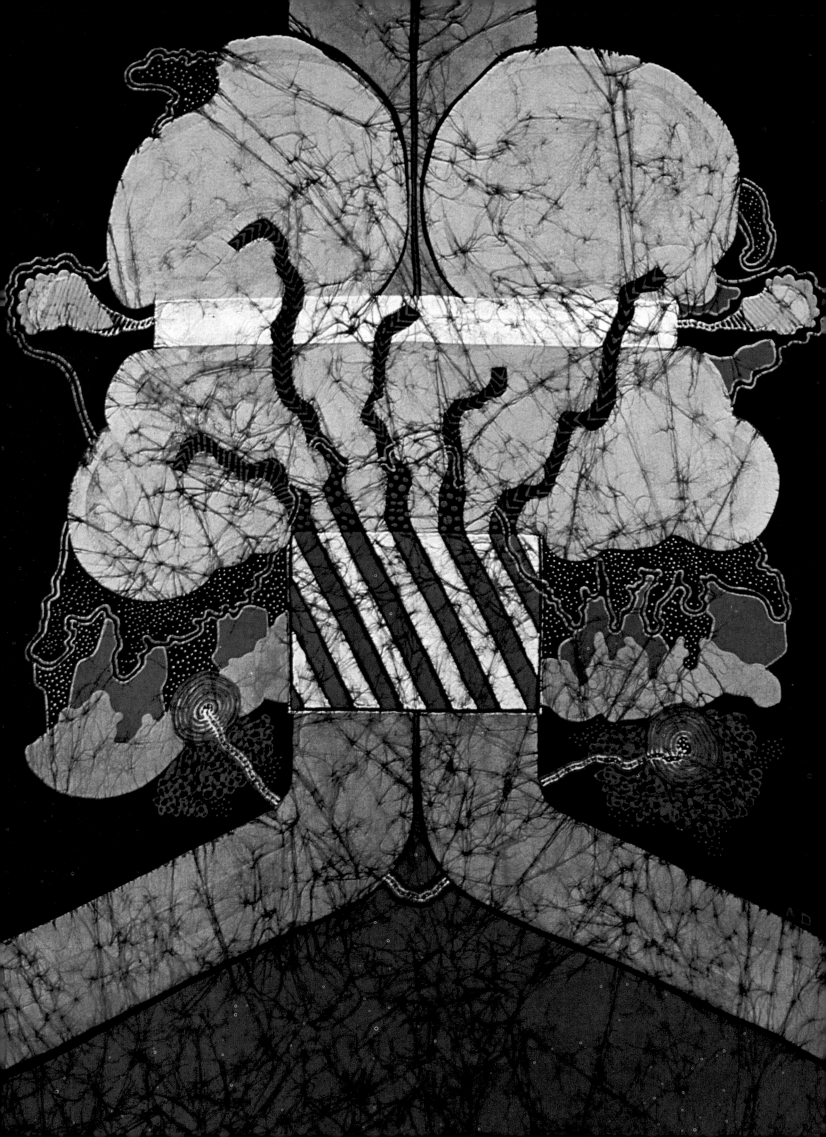

STEP-BY-STEP: MATERIALS

What you will need to start • where to find it • how to prepare
fabric and wax • how to arrange a working surface

This section describes what you need and why. At the end of this book there is a list of suggested places where you can obtain these materials. There are lists of suppliers and detailed recipes for mixing dye-colours.

Batik is traditionally done on either pure silk or cotton. Most synthetic fabrics will not accept cold water dyes, therefore natural fibres are best as they will accept every type of dye. Natural fibres include linen, wool and cloth made from jute or hemp such as hessian or burlap. Varieties of fabrics made with these fibres include muslin, cotton velveteen, corduroy, canvas, silk brocades and batiste. These are all suitable for batik. Of the synthetics; only viscose rayon can be dyed successfully.

Although the soft sheen of silk fabrics makes dye colours seem glossier than when applied to cotton, in fact silk absorbs less dye and produces a muted effect unless special dyes are used. Many professional batik artists prefer cotton to all other materials and the beginner is advised to use this material exclusively when experimenting. In this step-by-step section Noel Dyrenforth uses pure bleached cotton of the same weight and weave as a fairly strong handkerchief.

The first step in preparing any new material is to wash it thoroughly. Pure soap, in liquid, powder, or flake form is best for this purpose. Add a water softener, such as Calgon, while washing and rinsing. This makes the fabric more receptive to dye. Remember that cotton can be boiled, but silk cannot, since its brilliance will be lost. This wash also pre-shrinks new materials, which ensures that further washing will not alter the size of the finished batik. This is particularly important when making clothes, or

Left: A batik called *Don't talk* by Noel Dyrenforth. It demonstrates a variety of edges – crisp or crackly, straight or curved, taut or flabby – which the medium can produce. The order of dyeing was pale blue, followed by pink, deep orange and finally navy blue

designing a hanging to fit a standard size of frame or stretcher. Frames suitable for batik can be bought from many craft shops or batik supply dealers, either specially made, or ordered from a standard assortment. Alternatively, canvas stretchers available from art shops will serve the same purpose.

When the fabric has been washed and ironed it is time to start work. A later section on design shows methods of transferring ideas onto fabric. It is important to remember that the outer limits of the design should not overlap the inner edge of the frame, otherwise wax may glue fabric and frame together. The effect of stretching the fabric should be allowed for when considering this.

Some people don't bother to stretch the fabric at all. They may simply lay the material flat on a table which has been protected by a sheet of plastic or oil-cloth. The smooth shiny surface of these materials prevents the molten wax which penetrates the fabric sticking it onto the table.

If you intend to apply wax in broad, solid areas, or if you are making a precise pattern on the fabric, use a batik frame or stretcher. Each of the four sides of a batik frame is notched, and these notches interlock to make a wide variety of rectangular frame sizes. Stretching the fabric over this open frame has the additional advantage of allowing you to check that the wax is penetrating perfectly, by simply tipping the frame and letting the light shine through.

Stretching the fabric over the frame does not require any special skill, but it does need care and neatness. Lay the fabric out on a flat surface and put the assembled frame in the middle. Leave at least two inches of fabric as a border all around the outside edge of the frame. Begin to tack the fabric to the outside edge of the frame, starting in the middle of one of the longer sides. The second pinning should be made in the middle of the opposite side, and then the third and fourth are made at the centres of the remaining sides, pulling out the fabric to stretch it at each pinning. Keep following this regular pinning until the whole fabric is held taut.

The degree of tautness in the stretched fabric is hard to judge but becomes easier with practice. Obviously, the more open the weave and the larger the frame, the harder it is to keep the material taut throughout. The aim is to keep the fabric flat and smooth under working conditions. The fabric should be stretched tight enough to withstand the light pressure of brush or tjanting, about equal in weight to a full pack of cigarettes. This weight should depress the surface without leaving a permanent dent in it.

Now the stretched fabric, with the design lightly pencilled on it, is ready for the first waxing. To apply the wax you will need tjanting and brushes, an absorbent rag or kitchen paper to catch drips, and of course molten wax. Noel Dyrenforth's method of keeping wax at the right temperature involves a meat fondue pot on an electrically heated stand. The stand has a built-in thermostat which maintains the wax at about 55°C (130°F). An electric frying pan is equally suitable. If you are using a double boiler to heat the wax on the stove a kitchen thermometer should be used. The temperature should be maintained between 49°C (120°F) and 60°C (140°F). Below 49°C (120°F) the wax is not runny enough for easy use, and is less likely to penetrate the fabric satisfactorily. Above 60°C (140°F) the wax is likely to start smoking, which is both smelly and dangerous. Don't leave the hot wax unattended and keep bicarbonate of soda on hand in case the wax catches fire. After a while you will be able to judge the correct temperature by eye, since wax that is hot enough is translucent and has the consistency of milk.

Wax for batik can be paraffin wax or beeswax, or a mixture of the two. Beeswax is more pliable and is therefore excellent for drawing lines and fine details or for work requiring minimum crackle. For this reason many artists use pure beeswax for the first waxing. Paraffin wax is more brittle and results in a lot of crackle. Combinations of beeswax and paraffin wax yield varying results, the rule being that more paraffin produces more crackle. If you use a wax with a high proportion of paraffin wax you need to handle the fabric carefully to avoid unintentional crackling. Many art shops sell a special blend of wax, ready mixed in the right proportions for general batik use. There are no rules about crackle; it is a matter of personal taste and depends on what you want to make. It's useful to keep scraps of fabric handy, to test waxes and dyes while working. They will form a valuable record of your experiments in colour and pattern.

There are various methods for removing the wax from the finished batik. One requires a hot iron and a supply of newspaper. The second requires a pan large enough to boil the fabric in. The third method uses a large receptacle, such as the dye-bowl, containing sufficient cleaning fluid to cover the batik. The fourth method is the lazy one: dry-cleaning, but it is often a good idea to follow up the other methods with dry-cleaning to ensure that the wax has been completely removed.

Not only what you do, but how you do it, is a vital part of the preparation. Good workshop practice contributes just as much to the finished batik as the way you handle tjanting and brushes. With little experience you will be stretching the fabric perfectly without even thinking about it. Similarly it is important to plan the layout of the few simple tools so that all your attention can be concentrated on waxing the fabric and not on finding equipment. If the stretched fabric is large, it will be necessary either to turn the frame around on the table top, or to walk around the table itself to wax areas on the far edge. If this is the case put the pot containing the molten wax on a table where it will be within reach but not in danger of being upset. Batik is considerably less dangerous than cooking, but it needs the same kind of safety precautions.

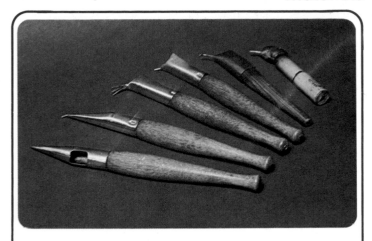

Above: Tjantings can be almost as varied as brushes in the effects they produce. This selection includes pen-like instruments which each produce a different width of waxed line, a triple-spouted tjanting which makes multiple marks and, on the far right, a Javanese tjanting with a short, stumpy handle suggesting closer control

Right and below: These are the standard materials for working in batik: **1** plastic bowl, **2** bleached cotton fabric, **3** thermostatically controlled electric stand with saucepan, **4** wide and narrow bristle brushes, **5** thermometer, **6** single-spout tjanting, **7** iron, **8** adjustable frame, **9** paraffin wax, **10** beeswax, **11** pack of wax granules specially made for batik, **12** tubs of fibre-reactive dye, **13** tacks, **14** plastic clothes pegs, **15** bottle of liquid detergent, **16** plastic container of cleaning fluid, **17** salt, **18** washing soda, **19** powdered urea and **20** rubber gloves. Ways of using ingredients will be found in the recipes on page 77

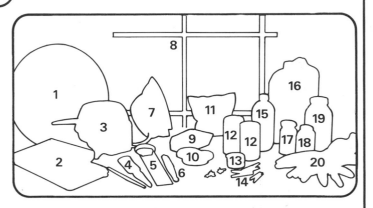

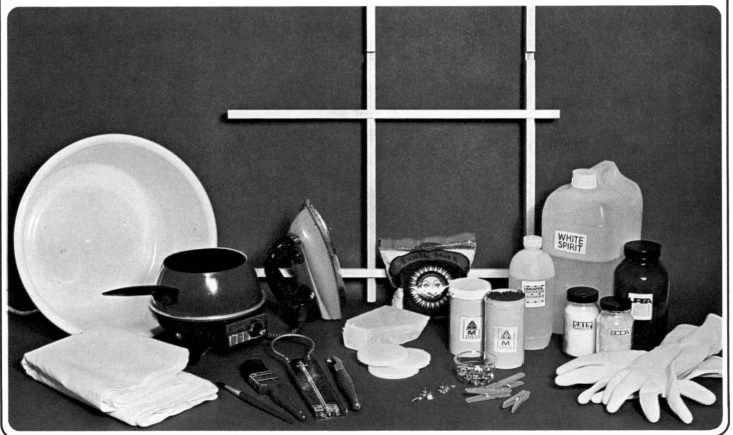

DESIGN AND INSPIRATION

Design ideas • transferring them to fabric • the use of colour

You will need: paper, soft pencils or charcoal, ruler, graph paper, carbon paper.

What to do: find materials to help your ideas flow such as natural objects, pebbles, flowers, leaf skeletons, sea shells or photographs that bring out the pattern and texture in fish scales, feathers, ferns, butterfly wings and so on.

These step-by-step sections invite you to accompany Noel Dyrenforth as he executes his design in batik. Unlike fabric printing, which builds up shapes and patterns by putting one colour on top of another, batik actually saturates the whole fabric with colour, and each dye-colour is physically absorbed by all the others.

Noel's designs are simple and schematic. He is only concerned with broad outlines and areas. The more subtle patterns and textures will be discovered while actually working with tjanting and brush. He normally transfers his designs onto the fabric by eye, preferring to redraw the spirit of an idea rather than stiffen a design by careful copying. When the character of a design depends on complicated detail, however, he does 'square-up' a drawing. This simply means drawing a grid of light pencil lines on top of the design, and drawing a proportionately larger grid onto the fabric. These grids are normally made up of squares, hence the expression 'square-up'. The grid system makes it easy to copy the design within a specific square onto the corresponding square on the fabric to reproduce the overall proportions of the design. Another method of transferring a drawing to the fabric is by using carbon paper, but this requires that your original drawing is done to the right size.

The waxing process in batik adds an extra dimension to design. Dyeing the fabric represents the positive process of adding and modifying colour. But waxing, in a special sense, is a negative process: it subtracts colour by resisting the action of the dye.

Below: Noel working on the original design for a one-colour batik. He concentrates on making the flower's silhouette as clear and interesting as possible by dividing the petals into contrasting groups of fat and thin, angular and curved. The placing of the design within the rectangle is equally important. Working with a simple design in one colour shows the fundamental 'resist' effect of batik

Left: To transfer the design from paper to fabric, a sheet of dressmaker's carbon paper is sandwiched between the two. The three layers are pinned or clipped to a table or drawing board to keep them in place, and the drawing is traced with a soft pencil so that the design comes through to the fabric

Below left: Painting molten wax onto the stretched fabric ensures that the areas covered will resist the dye and remain white in the finished batik. Care is taken to wax inside the drawn outline of the flower so that these lines will be covered by dye and disappear

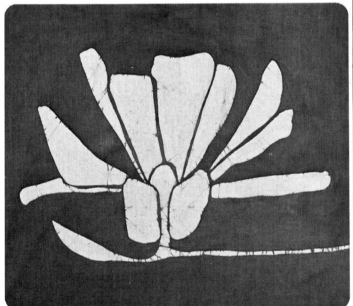

Top: The areas to remain white in the finished batik have been painted with wax which looks grey in the picture. The surrounding white unwaxed areas will be darkened by dye. This reversal process of adding wax to subtract fabric from the effect of the dye is the basic principle of batik

Above: The fabric has been dyed and dried, and the wax has been removed. These two pictures illustrate the basic reversal process, from dark wax on white fabric to white fabric defined by dark dye

As you add each new area of wax, you are painting with the *previous* dye-colour, while unwaxed shapes and patterns. will be affected by the *next* dye-colour. When you add wax you are subtracting that particular area from all the subsequent dye-colours. Thus batik can be thought of in the same way as a photographic process, with each waxing creating a negative image, which is developed when the next dye-colour darkens the fabric, the image being defined by the lighter areas.

It is important to keep several characteristics of batik in mind when designing so that your ideas will harmonize with its distinctive properties. The first of these is transparency: everything shows. So if you make a mistake or regret waxing an area, it is advisable to modify your design there and then so that an error becomes absorbed as a bonus. Sometimes Noel Dyrenforth spills or spatters some wax on an area he intended to leave blank. He studies the mistake' in terms of how it affects existing rhythms and patterns. Then he may choose to repeat this accident three or four times to build up a new pattern.

In a similar way, the relationship between colours and their tone, their degree of lightness or darkness, is not precisely controllable in batik. This lends a vital spontaneity to the process of design; an element of experiment and discovery is always present. Noel Dyrenforth recommends the colour combinations shown on page 26 for you to try. Dye-colours depend on many factors such as dye concentration, dyeing time and the nature of the fabric, but these charts will give a general indication of what will happen in the final batik. Two light colours, in producing a third, will darken much more than you might expect. It is this rich blending effect that makes tonal prediction with dyes so difficult.

The key to designing a multiple dye batik is to gain a reasonable knowledge of the colour and tone changes that will take place as each colour is added. Experience is a good, general guide, especially when supported by a notebook recording the proportions

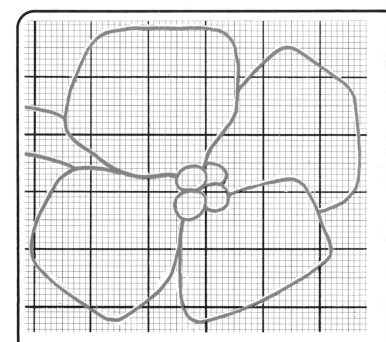

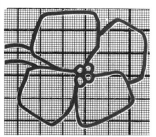

Above: As most people prefer to work on batiks which are larger than the paper used for the drawing, it is necessary to blow up the designs. The best and simplest way to enlarge (or reduce) a design is to make a graph pattern. This shows where lines have to be drawn on the larger scale, occupying the corresponding squares. The squares must be drawn very lightly onto the fabric so that they do not show through the finished batik. Sketching the design on sheets of graph paper made for this purpose will save time and effort

This page: Photographs are good sources of design motifs because they have already reduced objects to flat patterns, but the same transformation is possible by cutting shapes out of a piece of cardboard and using the resultant frame to isolate and emphasize sections of your vision. Lay this frame on a rough wood surface or even on parts of colour photographs and strong images emerge. The rock crystals, butterfly, fern and seashell shown here are examples of designs from nature which can be stylized into a batik pattern. Just looking through any picture book can start ideas flowing

Design and Inspiration

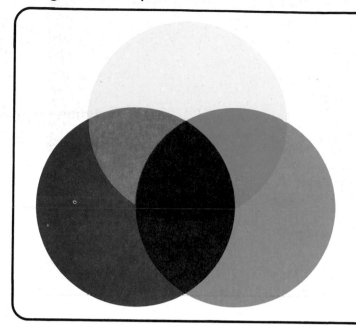

of past dye mixtures. Fortunately, there is plenty of leeway in the dyeing process to make up for the difficulty in predicting the exact tint of a dye. Batiks are normally dyed from the lightest to the darkest colour so that the darkest tones are built up gradually. This sequence leaves the darkest dye until last to smooth out any jarring tonal contrasts.

The best way to control colour and tone effects is to keep a sample of testing dyes and overdyeing on a separate strip of fabric. This is an excellent guide while working, and if accompanied by brief notes on colour mixtures, order of dyeing, and length of time in the dye bath, you will quickly build up a sample book to guide future experiments.

Design is rooted in the real world of observation. Choosing suitable outlines and tones from nature involves a complex process of selection and emphasis. Today there is a wealth of easily available two-dimensional materials such as reproductions of paintings, photographs and film stills, all of which present ideas to incorporate with your own designs. The illustrations on page 25 are images drawn from nature and are already partially stylized. Their pattern element has been emphasized, exaggerated and almost separated from reality.

Noel Dyrenforth's work is a marvellous example of this process in action. Project 1 in this book reveals how the gradual addition of abstract elements can produce a batik which is something more than a mere pattern. Noel locks together elements which are quite contradictory in shape and character.

Having chosen to develop an idea in four colours, the most frequently made error in batik is to redraw the whole design with the first one or two waxings. This always gives the finished batik a meagre look, as though a pair of coloured drawings had merely been superimposed. The skill lies in blending the different waxings and dyeings in the finished batik so that it is almost impossible for anyone but the artist to know the number or the order of dyes used.

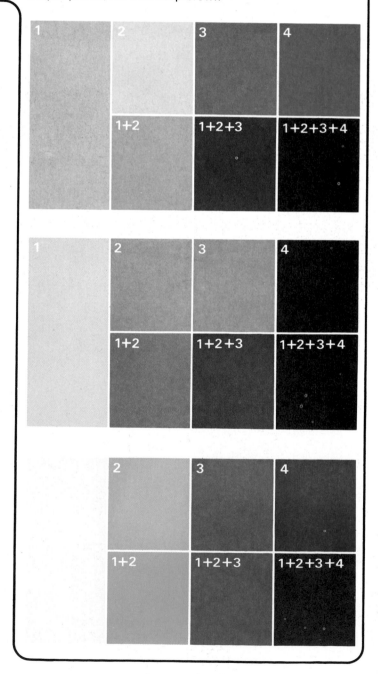

PROJECT 1: A WALL-HANGING

A complete batik, step-by-step, from blank fabric •
four waxings and dyeings • using tjantings and brushes •
using the dye bath • removing the wax • stretching

You will need: the materials shown on page 21.
What to do: wash and iron fabric—transfer design
onto fabric—stretch fabric on frame—melt wax and
apply it to fabric with tjanting and brush—remove
fabric from frame—mix dye and immerse fabric in
dye bath wearing rubber gloves—lift wet fabric onto
absorbent paper and then hang it on a line to dry
overnight—repeat process for each colour—remove
wax from fabric—finally restretch fabric.

Wall-hangings present the best opportunities for
expressing yourself with batik and for experimenting
with the various techniques available. This project
will demonstrate clearly the basic techniques that
Noel Dyrenforth uses in most of his work, and the way
in which a planned sequence of waxing and dyeing
builds up into a finished work. The methods demonstrated here are fundamental to batik and are often
re-used in the other projects in this book.

When you begin your batik make sure that all the
equipment is laid out so that you can reach all of the
fabric comfortably. Place the pot of hot wax on the
right-hand side of the frame (if you're right-handed).
Lay out the tjantings and the brushes in front of the
wax pot. Keep at least one rag there to mop up any
drips or splashes of wax. A small piece of heavy
cardboard is also useful to catch any drips from the
tjanting as you move it across to the fabric.

The tjanting is purpose-built for batik. Some
hundreds of years of development guarantee its
effectiveness as the simplest way to decorate the
fabric. This instrument is best when you want to
create lines and dots; it is perfect for outlining areas
precisely and adding highlights. Hold it as you would
a pen, dip it carefully into the molten wax to fill the
reservoir and let any excess wax drip back into the pot.
Transfer the tjanting to the fabric, holding the cardboard drip tray or a rag underneath the spout. Draw
the tjanting smoothly towards you across the fabric.
If the wax is the correct temperature it will look as

Above: The first step in actually doing batik is to melt the
wax and keep it molten while you work. One possible way
to do this is in an electric pot with a thermostatic control,
placed on an asbestos mat. A double boiler works well too
but needs to be checked with a thermometer to keep the
wax between 49°C (120°F) and 60°C (140°F). Electric
frying pans or fondue pots are also good ideas

Right: Noel working on the first waxing of the wall-hanging.
The inset is Noel's working drawing for this project. The
main lines of the composition and its colour scheme are
roughly indicated, but there is no intention to predict the
effect of the finished batik. The first waxing will not repeat
all the lines shown here but only those details that will be
kept white throughout. The order of dyeing will be pale pink,
brilliant yellow, medium blue and finally navy blue. Noel is
shown midway through the first waxing when everything
except the broad chevron shape, which was waxed with a
brush, has been drawn in with different tjantings. The wax
shows up clearly against the white cotton and the straight
waxed lines on the right demonstrate the tautness of the
fabric stretched on the frame

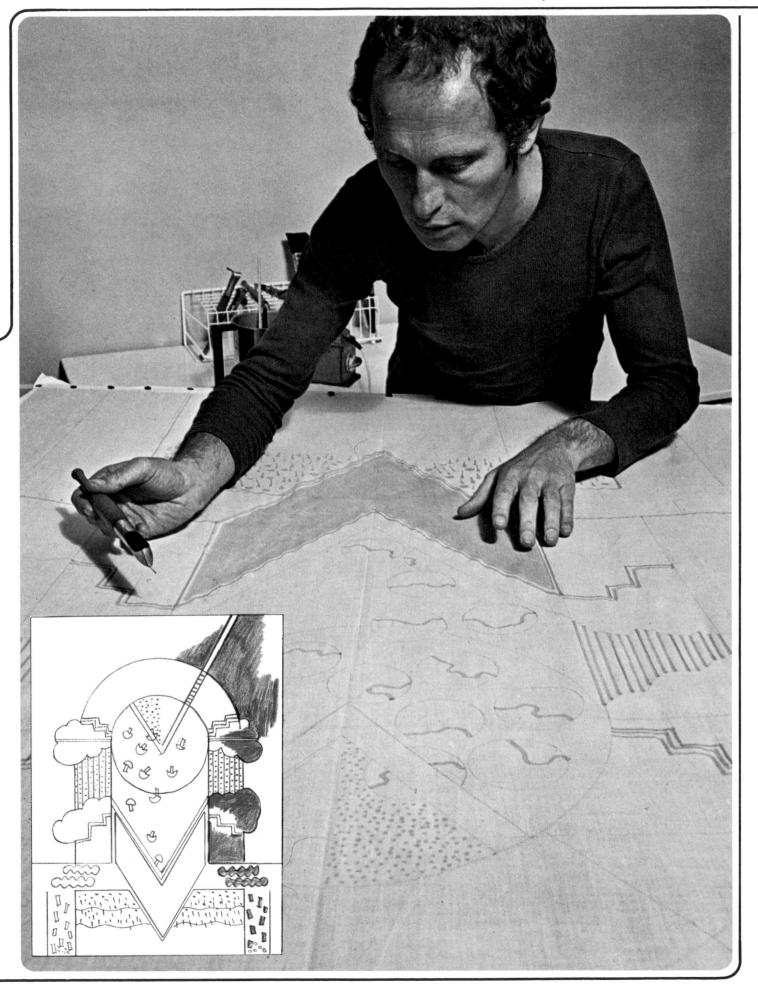

though the fabric is pulling it out of the spout. The wax will sink into the fabric, spreading slightly, and becoming transparent. If it remains opaque, the wax is too cool and is only lying on the surface of the fabric — it is important to ensure that the wax penetrates completely or it will not resist the dye. This transparency is essential. Keeping the wax flowing smoothly will regulate the speed with which you use the tjanting. Try drawing dotted lines using the cardboard drip tray as a guard by laying it on the fabric to mark the end of a stroke. By this time, even if you've been working quickly, the wax in the reservoir of the tjanting will be too cool. Dip the tjanting back in the pot. Hold it there for a few seconds to recharge and reheat the wax.

Brushes, once dipped in wax, change their nature to become smooth, slithery instruments. Therefore, the stiffer the brush, the more character each stroke will have. The brush will have to be recharged more often than a tjanting, but will, of course, cover more fabric with each stroke. Use the brush for texture by turning it in your fingers as you move it across the fabric. This will vary the width of the line and vary the quality of the edge, from clear-cut to fuzzy, from a hard line to one where individual curls of wax jut out. Recharge the brush for each stroke; the hot wax must flow onto and into the fabric as a thin, transparent fluid.

Noel Dyrenforth has developed a large range of brush strokes and many variations are possible during experimentation. The most important factor is to remember how to create the overall effect; it is very easy to be hypnotized by the easy way different textures develop. If they grow more important than the design then the result will be a mush of colour.

Noel has laid out his design for this project and will develop it through four waxings, each one to be followed by a different dye-colour. The order of dyeing planned for this batik starts with pink, followed by yellow, a medium blue and finally navy

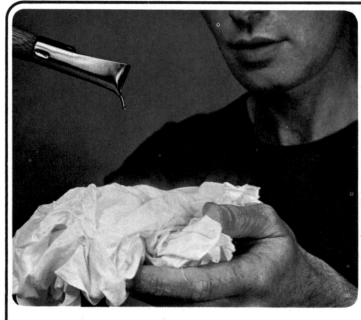

Above: A pad of cloth or absorbent paper is essential to catch drips of hot wax as the refilled brush or tjanting is moved from wax pot to fabric. You should be as decisive as possible and move quickly to the fabric. If wax does drip from the tjanting or brush, the best solution is to incorporate the 'mistake' into the final design

Right: Filling in the large shape of the chevron with a brush. There are no rules for handling molten wax with a brush; it can be used flat to cover a large area with wax or sideways to produce a narrower line. Do not fill the brush too full, or the wax will drip before it reaches the fabric, and don't brush back and forth, housepainter style. If a single stroke does not make a waxy streak, it means either that there is not enough wax on the brush, or that the wax is not hot enough. In either case dip the brush in the molten wax again. When wax is correctly applied to the fabric it looks dark and transparent because it has penetrated the cloth

Below: This straight-spouted tjanting is used as freely as a pen, but like a pen, it cannot be pushed forward and away from you or the spout will catch in the fibres and could go through the cloth. Natural wrist movements from side to side and backwards work well. Hardly any downward pressure is needed because as long as the wax is hot it will keep flowing at a controlled rate. The tjanting must keep moving once in contact with the fabric. A pause for thought can lead to a puddle of wax, so you should always know what you want to do before applying the tjanting to the fabric

Above: The first waxing completed. Dark areas show which parts are waxed, and these will be bare fabric in the finished batik. When you do the first waxing you are essentially 'painting' in white and these areas will be highlights

Below: The still wet fabric after the first dye bath looks darker and more brilliant than the pale pink of the dye. The fabric has been lifted out of the dye while it was still wet, and quickly put onto sheets of newspaper to absorb excess dye. It is then hung up to dry and Noel is shown here using a cloth to mop up drops of excess dye. This prevents the dye collecting on the waxed areas

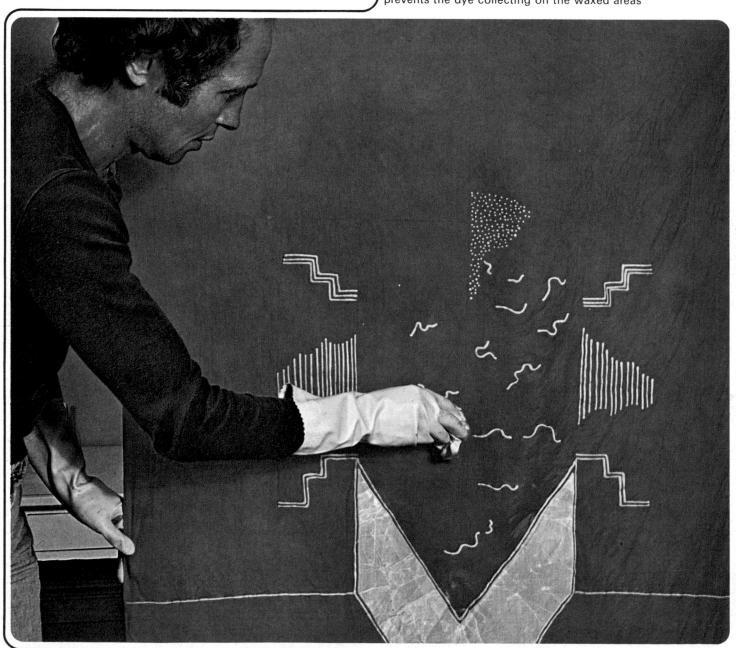

Left: During the second waxing Noel gives a soft, furry edge to this area by using the brush with a delicate sweeping action and lifting it off the fabric sharply at the end of each stroke. Various effects are possible with brushes, and it can be fun to experiment

Centre left: The tjanting can be used very effectively to make small dots. It should just be held on the fabric for a fraction of a second however, or the dot will spread into a puddle

Bottom left: Small brushes are used for delicate touches even though the brush will have to be repeatedly dipped in the wax pot. The steady flow of wax sets the pace, and trying to make a tiny mark with the corner of a large brush will only cause blots

Above: The second waxing completed. The areas waxed during the first waxing are white, having resisted all dye-colour. The second waxing has covered areas of the light pink fabric so that these will resist further dyeing

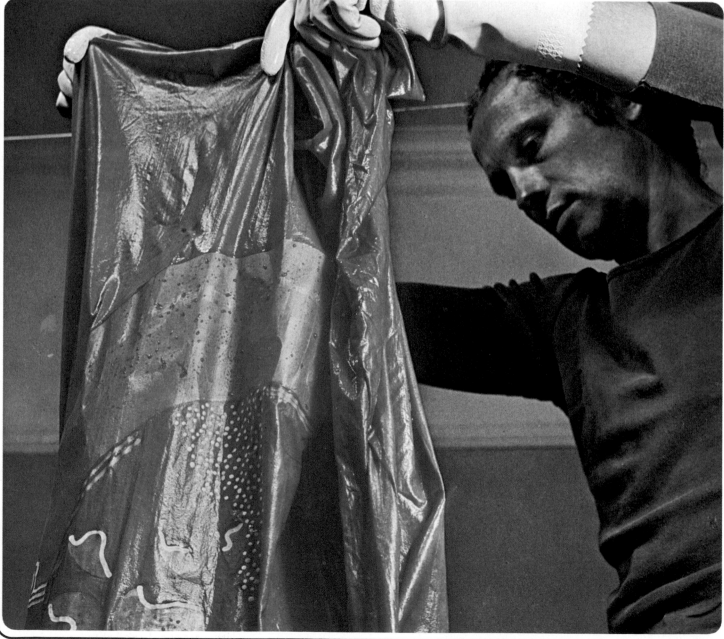

Far left: The second dyeing is with a brilliant yellow dye. Submerge the fabric thoroughly to allow the dye to penetrate the cloth having first made sure there is enough dye solution in the bowl to cover the fabric. Handle the cloth gently and let it swim freely in the dye bath, turning it frequently during the 15 to 30 minute dyeing period. It is always best to use rubber gloves during the dyeings

Below left: Lifting the fabric slowly out of the dye bath Noel lets the dye run back into the bowl and checks that it has taken evenly. Then he lays the cloth flat on sheets of newspaper and mops the surface gently with an absorbent cloth before hanging the fabric on a line to dry

Left: With fibre-reactive dyes, the dye-colour fixes itself to the fibres during the drying period, which is about 12 hours under normal household conditions. Any dye that is trapped on the waxed areas might later be ironed into the cloth. To prevent this, wipe the fabric gently but thoroughly on both sides

Above: After the second dyeing, the brilliant yellow has added to the pink to give a luminous orange colour. Areas of this orange will be covered by the third waxing. Meanwhile the areas of fabric already sealed in wax can be seen clearly as pink or white

blue. The recipes for these cold water dyes using either Dylon, Procion M or other dye-colours are given on page 77.

Obviously the way the fabric is dyed has a vital effect on the final appearance of the batik. As some parts of the fabric will be stiff with wax, care in handling is essential. First wet the cloth. Make sure that there is sufficient liquid to cover the fabric in the dye bath. It should remain there for anything from 15 to 30 minutes or longer, depending on the strength of colour desired and the concentration of the dye. Fold the fabric loosely and lower it gently into the dye bath. Squash the bundle gently against the bottom of the bowl, applying slow, firm pressure. Rotate the fabric in the bowl to make sure that the dye penetrates evenly. To remove the fabric, hold it by the ends of one edge and lift straight up, letting excess dye run back into the bowl. Then open the fabric out fully and lay it flat on top of several layers of newspaper. Pat it carefully all over with an absorbent cloth, soaking up more of the surface dye. Finally, hang the fabric from a line by one edge and gently wipe both sides with absorbent paper to remove the few remaining drops of dye which will have collected at the upper edges of waxed areas. This elaborate blotting and wiping is important. Any dye which has not been absorbed by the fabric could run down during drying, leaving dark disfiguring stripes and stains. Fixation — the chemical linkage between dye and fibre — takes place as the fabric dries. In a warm humid atmosphere fixation can be complete in two to three hours. But complete drying will take much longer in normal room temperature. Drying outdoors is ideal provided the fabric is kept out of strong sunlight or strong winds.

The first waxing has a special importance because the wax traps white fabric. As in watercolour painting the highlights have to be planned and preserved before the more weighty business of colour and tone can be dealt with. Noel's highlights are sparingly

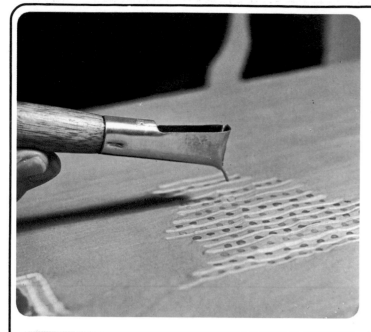

Far left: During the third waxing it is easy to see the way that the multi-coloured effects of the finished batik are created, successive waxings fitting together like a jig-saw puzzle. Here the tjanting is used to wax and retain areas of orange fabric as delicate dots

Left: The steady flow of the molten wax from the full width of the brush invites firm, confident handling. When the wax stops running freely it means that it is too cool to penetrate the fabric and the instrument must be dipped into the wax pot to reheat and refill

Below left: Noel is preserving the soft, furry edge he created during the second waxing by covering the whole area with a further layer of wax. Notice that he always holds a cloth for catching drips. During each waxing Noel constantly looks for cracks in the previously waxed areas, caused by handling the fabric. Any he sees are waxed again to prevent dye-colour penetrating at this stage

Above: The third waxing complete. Selected areas of orange fabric have been covered and will be unaffected by the next dye bath. Waxed areas appear darker than they will in the finished wall-hanging after the wax has been removed

distributed in a rough symmetry at the centre of the fabric. His intention is to create a rich, sonorous batik, demonstrating the maximum depth of colour and tone. Clearly, large areas of white fabric would dilute this richness.

A much greater proportion of the pink fabric is waxed in the second waxing. The overall pink dye helps to unify all subsequent colours, lending a little warmth to even the coldest overdye, and preventing those pink areas now being locked in wax from appearing too isolated in the finished batik. The tiny dots and the even, delicate lines of the tjanting are preserving tiny parts of the pink fabric. Although these areas will be almost invisible in the finished batik, as they will be overlaid with a dark crackle, and although they have no major part to play in the composition, they nevertheless add sparkle to the massive, more bland areas.

The second colour is a brilliant yellow, which may appear lighter in tone than the preceding pink, thus seeming to contradict the light to dark rule of colour sequences. But a brilliant yellow is the most luminous of all colours. If it had been applied first to the bleached white cotton its brilliance would have swamped every other colour. By applying it second, Noel has reduced its sting with the duller, pink dye already on the fabric. The third waxing locks up the orange colour resulting from the blend of pink and yellow. The layers of glossy wax magnify the brilliance of the colours that they enclose. Obviously dye does not affect these waxed areas and they can function as a check on the required strength of the next dye.

The wetness of the freshly dyed fabric always disguises the actual intensity of the dye, but generally you can assume that the apparent strength of dye on wet fabric is about double its actual strength. Fortunately the same principle applies to the colour of the dry fabric isolated and intensified by a layer of wax. As the waxed layer should normally be a lighter

Above: The third dyeing complete with the fabric dried and restretched. The medium blue dye has combined with the orange to create a soft brown. Throughout this sequence of waxing and dyeing all the unwaxed areas have become progressively darker

Left: In the fourth and final waxing, almost all the background is waxed over with a broad brush. Only the central area and narrow areas around the main forms will be exposed to the final dye. The solid layer of wax over the fabric will be crackled to admit the navy blue dye and create a finely marbled effect covering almost the whole batik

Below: It is always best to create a careful outline of an area with a small brush before filling it in with a larger one. Noel is increasing the tautness of the fabric by pressing down lightly with his forefinger. This helps him to keep an even pressure on the brush and a sharp edge to the curve he is painting. This edge must be accurate as he is trying to leave a thin arc of fabric free between this brush stroke and the edge of the wax-covered pink area

tone than the wet dye it is advisable to leave the fabric in the dye bath until the wet areas are obviously darker in tone and richer in colour than the waxed sections.

During the next waxing Noel ensures that cracks which may have appeared in the already waxed areas are covered once again with wax. If he ignored them they would take the third dye-colour and become dark gashes in the lighter colours and not simply crackle.

The third colour is a cold, medium blue. Having laid a foundation of bright colour and preserved pink, orange and white areas, he can afford to damp down the orange warmth everywhere else. As well as adding to the main structure with each of the three waxings he has been consistent in maintaining the lighter patterns of dashes, dots, and lines which allow each colour to breathe through the next one.

When the fourth waxing is complete, almost the whole of the fabric is shiny on both sides with a wax crust. Noel then crumples this crust to allow the final dark blue dye to crackle through the wax, and vein all the other colours. Although the crackle is created by crumpling the fabric in a regular way, the character and pattern of the crackle is partly dictated by the manner in which the wax was originally applied. Noel is very careful to brush wax smoothly around the contour of each shape. Even when large areas of wax are being brushed on, he paints with long, parallel strokes to minimize the build-up of wax where brush strokes overlap. If thick slabs of wax do develop, the crackle effect may be very patchy. Large flakes of wax may break off the surface of the fabric, allowing whole areas to be dyed solid where only veining was intended.

After the four applications of wax and four different dye-colours, the design is complete. The fabric is crusted and weighty with layers of wax which must now be removed to reveal the final effect. The simplest way to remove the wax is with a hot iron. You will

Below left: Noel waxes over the finer details of the brown fabric he wants to keep after the final dye

Left: In the final inspection of the heavily waxed fabric, Noel once again checks for waxed areas that may have been crackled too much and retouches them with molten wax. This checking and retouching is done even at the end of this final waxing. Although he is planning to crackle all the wax before the final dyeing, he prefers to control the timing and distribution of the crackle

Above: The fourth waxing completed. The fabric is almost completely covered by wax. The heavier the wax, the more pronounced the crackle effect will be

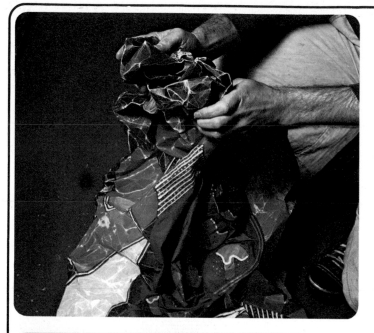

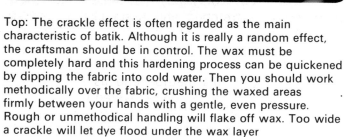

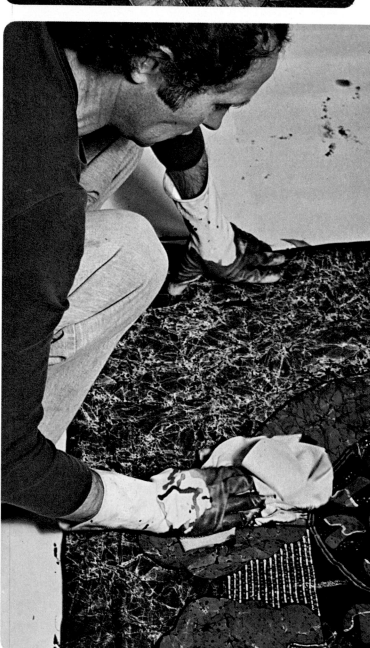

Top: The crackle effect is often regarded as the main characteristic of batik. Although it is really a random effect, the craftsman should be in control. The wax must be completely hard and this hardening process can be quickened by dipping the fabric into cold water. Then you should work methodically over the fabric, crushing the waxed areas firmly between your hands with a gentle, even pressure. Rough or unmethodical handling will flake off wax. Too wide a crackle will let dye flood under the wax layer

Above: All the waxed areas have been crackled to let the final navy blue dye marble the colours underneath. The few unwaxed areas now form a very dark background made by the effect of four dye baths. It is important to lift the fabric out of the bowl during dyeing to check the effect on the crackled areas. This effect can be seen most clearly in the white areas covered during the first waxing

Below: When the fabric is removed from the dye bath, Noel moves very quickly to lay it on layers of newspaper to absorb the excess dye. He blots the drops of dye which are trapped in the crackled wax. Speed is essential at this stage of every dyeing to prevent patchiness which can only be seen when the dye has dried

Left: The final wiping and blotting of the fabric with an absorbent cloth or paper towel. The white areas show the marbled effect of the dark dye

also need a lot of newspaper and a blanket which should be kept specially for this purpose. Cover the ironing board or table with this blanket and lay three or four sheets of newspaper on top. Then spread the batik over this and cover with three or four sheets of newspaper. The paper must be at least a week old or the print will be damp enough to stain the batik. Then simply iron the wax out of the batik and into the newspaper. As you iron, dark patches of wax will appear through the top layer of newspaper. As this happens, discard these waxy sheets from above and below the batik, replace them with fresh ones and continue to iron. Repeat this process until most of the wax is melted out of the batik. The more frequently you replace the newspaper, the quicker the whole process will be.

Some batik artists prefer to leave a small quantity of wax in the fabric both to stiffen it and to enrich the colours. This works very well when the batik is going to be restretched and hung like a painting. Although the ironing method is the one most often used, the wax can also be dissolved out of cotton fabrics by boiling. A large pan and constant stirring is the essence of this method and its advantage is that most of the wax can be recovered from the pan, though you may still have to iron out a small residue from the fabric. Another method is to submerge the fabric in cleaning fluid, having ironed out as much wax as possible between sheets of newspaper. Make sure that the bowl of cleaner is stored and used in a well-ventilated room and never exposed to an open flame. The simplest, though the most expensive method is to have the fabric dry-cleaned. Noel uses this as a final method of ensuring that all the wax has been removed.

The wall-hanging is finally re-ironed and put on stretchers ready to be hung. The final presentation of the batik is very important and always deserves thought. Noel prefers to leave his batiks without frames but framing can add a lot to some designs.

Project 1: A Wall-Hanging

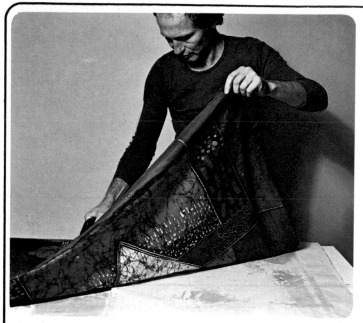

Left: The final step in batik is the removal of the wax. This can be done by ironing the fabric between layers of newspaper. Here Noel is lifting the fabric to check that wax is being absorbed into the paper underneath. Both the top and bottom layers must be changed as soon as the paper is saturated with wax and before the wax has time to reharden

Below: As the hot iron passes over the paper the shapes of the melting wax emerge. The heat of the iron also helps to fix the dye. Any residue of wax still in the fabric after ironing can be removed by immersing the cloth in a bowl of cleaning fluid (in a well-ventilated room) or by dry-cleaning. A final rinse in slightly soapy water will remove any residual cleaner or excess dye. Rinse and iron the batik before restretching it

Right: The finished wall-hanging. Despite the all-over crackle which Noel gave to the waxed areas before the final dye, most of the fine lines drawn with the tjanting have stayed sharp because beeswax was used for these details. A mixture of beeswax and paraffin wax was used for the rest of the work, and this produces a greater crackle effect

PROJECT 2: A CUSHION COVER

Direct painting of dyes onto the fabric
within waxed boundaries

You will need: fabric cushion cover, wax, tjanting, dyes, thickening agent, dye bath, various brushes.
What to do: transfer the design onto the fabric—use the tjanting to outline design in wax—thicken each dye-colour with a commercial thickening agent (see page 78 for recipe)—paint inside wax outlines—brush wax evenly over all painted areas—gently crackle the wax and immerse fabric in dye bath—hang fabric to dry—remove wax.

The technique of direct painting exploits the same principle of wax-resisting dye as the previous project. This method, however, allows any number of colours to be applied at the same working session, by painting them directly onto the surface of the fabric. Fabrics decorated by direct painting are not usually reversible unless they are very thin. This painted dye will only penetrate such materials as fine cotton lawn and sheer silk. Noel Dyrenforth is making a cushion cover using this technique. Designing for the direct painting technique is similar to planning the patchwork areas of stained glass. This is how Noel approaches the problem, by exaggerating outline and flattening form to invent the most expressive and decorative shapes. The tjanting is the ideal instrument for outlining this design, once it has been transferred to the fabric. The character of the waxed line is very important but should not vary too much or it will tend to appear more important than the painted areas.

Filling in the colours is easy as all the edges are already defined. Normal dye-mix is too runny for direct painting, so the recipe on page 78 describes how to thicken the dye. Remember to use a separate, clean brush for each colour.

As Noel wants the cushion to have crackle effect, he brushes a thin layer of wax over the fabric when the colours have dried. He then crumples this gently to crack the wax and immerses it in a normal dye bath. Finally the wax is removed by ironing, a cushion is inserted, and the cover closed with Velcro.

Far left, top: The first step in the direct painting technique is to outline the entire design in wax using a tjanting. A brush could be used to create wider lines. These lines of wax define areas of fabric which can then be painted with dyes of various colours. This method is called direct dyeing as the colour is applied to the fabric without immersion in a dye bath

Far left, bottom: The dye-colours, each slightly thickened to a more paint-like consistency (see recipe on page 78), are painted into the wax enclosures which ensure a crisp edge to each colour section

Left: When all the dye-colours are dry, Noel paints the entire fabric with molten wax. When this has hardened he will crackle the wax and paint very dark colour over the crackle

Below: The finished cushion. Noel gave the layer of wax a very fine-veined crackle so that this effect would not confuse the clear shapes of the design

PROJECT 3: A LAMPSHADE

Stamping wax onto fabric • household articles that can be used as stamps

You will need: fabric, wax, lampshade frame—objects for stamping wax onto fabric like keys, tin cans, kitchen utensils etc.—thin sheet of foam rubber and sheet of plastic or oil cloth—pair of pliers, rubber gloves—small piece of foam rubber inside wax pot to act as a pad.

What to do: cut fabric to fit lampshade frame—stamp molten wax onto fabric using desired shapes—dye fabric by immersion—lift fabric onto newspaper and hang to dry overnight—repeat process for each colour—remove wax from fabric—assemble lampshade by stitching fabric to card and glueing to frame.

Any clearly defined shape that will hold and transfer hot wax is suitable for stamping wax onto fabric. The level of hot wax in the wax pot should be reduced, with a pad at the bottom which should rise slightly above the wax level. This absorbs the hot wax, so that stamps pressed on it will pick up wax evenly. The fabric should have the same quality of resilience, and in order to ensure this Noel has covered his work table with a sheet of thin foam rubber. On top of this, he has placed a sheet of oil cloth to protect the rubber from the hot wax and to prevent the wax from sticking the fabric to the working surface. The fabric to be stamped is placed on top.

Noel is making a lampshade using these stamping techniques. He has selected a frame made of two separate wire circles, which will be glued to the top and bottom of the plain cardboard which reinforces the finished fabric. This two-piece frame does away with vertical bars that would cast a shadow through the fabric shade. Any design of lampshade can be adapted to batik, as long as the design is considered with the shape in mind. Noel puts considerable weight on each stamp to achieve the crispest impression possible. The three dye baths are closely related in colour, warm blues and mauve, to emphasize the shadowy repetition of the stamped units.

Below: A selection of suitable tools for stamping fabric with hot wax. They are: a cork, a metal tube, two blocks of wood with nails hammered into them to form a pattern, a piece of rag tied around a dowel, a bent pipe cleaner, another cloth-wrapped stick, a triangle of felt glued to wood with a wooden handle nailed to it, a wooden block, and a pastry-cutter. There are many such household objects that can be used to stamp wax onto fabric. Deciding what to use is governed by whether or not the object will make a clear shape which can be built into a pattern, and whether the object is absorbent or heat-conducting

Opposite page, top left: When using the stamping technique on unstretched fabric, a sheet of oil cloth should be put underneath the fabric to stop molten wax from sticking it to the table. For this project it also helps to place a sheet of foam rubber under the oil cloth as the stamps will make a clearer impression on a resilient surface

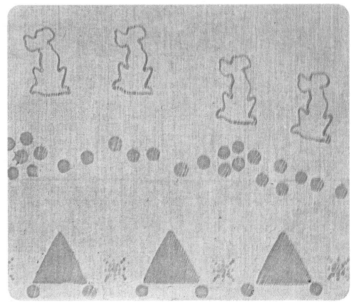

Top right: When stamping outlines in wax with a metal pastry-cutter, use pliers and a cloth. This is necessary with any metal stamps as they will otherwise conduct the heat of the wax and become too hot to hold

Above left: To make sure that the base of the stamping tool is evenly covered in wax, a piece of foam rubber can be put in the pot. This should protrude just above the level of the molten wax and act in the same way as an ink-pad when the stamps are pressed onto it

Above right: After waxing the patterns made by the stamps begin to build up. The reason for using stamps is to be able to repeat shapes, and simple patterns do this most effectively. For first attempts it is easier to mark out the repeat sequence on the fabric as a working guide so that stamps can be applied at regular intervals. Noel wants this pattern to be less regular, however, and he is improvising in irregular rhythms

Above left: Noel uses three waxings and dyeings in this project, but he uses the same stamps throughout so that the shapes crowd together but are defined by different colours in the finished batik

Above: Even the simplest shape like a circular cork can be used to produce a variety of effects. Here Noel uses it to stamp a disc of molten wax over an area that has already been waxed and dyed. In the finished batik these circles will frame colours and shapes created by the previous waxings. To keep the stamped shapes crisp and clear you must be decisive. Take the stamp to the fabric, press for a second and then lift it vertically clear

Left: The fuzzy edges to the marks made by the pipe cleaner provide a contrast to the crispness of the other stamps

Right: The finished lampshade in use. The fabric is simply backed with plain card and glued around the edges of two wire circles. There are no vertical wires to cast shadows through the batik's pleasing translucent patterns

PROJECT 4: WORKING ON PAPER

Cold wax on paper • wax rubbings using different textures found in the home

Drawing with cold wax

You will need: paper, cold liquid wax, watercolours or water soluble inks, soft paint brush, icing bag or plastic syringe.

What to do: use the icing bag or syringe to put cold liquid wax onto the paper in a pattern—paint a wash of colour across the pattern to reveal all its shape and texture—rub or scrape off the wax.

Rubbing textures with wax

You will need: paper, a candle or wax crayons, watercolours or water soluble inks, soft paint brush, cellophane tape — objects with raised textures or relief patterns.

What to do: tape paper firmly over textured object and rub evenly across the paper with the candle or crayon—remove paper and paint a wash of colour across the wax to expose the texture.

This technique can be incorporated with others in large-scale batiks as a 'quote' from the real world. It is often successful using paper or fabric. Noel demonstrates wax rubbing against a cast-iron moulding from an old stove, a textile printing block and a section of a spiky twig. The wash exposes the original textures of the surface in negative form, defined against the colour.

The secret of a crisp, clear image is to attach the paper or cloth to be dyed firmly to the textured object. Stretch the material around, or across, as taut as possible and secure it with cellophane tape. Rub the wax — either a candle, crayon or a piece of wax — briskly and evenly across the fabric. If you do it too slowly, or vary the pressure, the wax will dip into the hollows and obliterate the image.

A few suggestions for suitable objects are: decorative mouldings in wood, plaster or metal, wire grills from refrigerators and ovens, braided matting, woven basket work, cast-iron drain covers, and the most obvious one, brass rubbings.

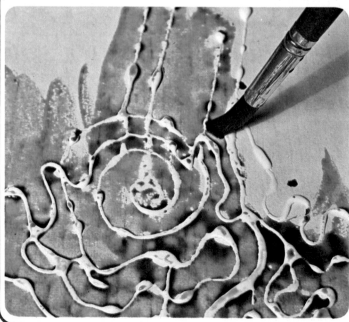

Top left: An icing bag or syringe is a quick and accurate way to squeeze cold liquid wax onto any surface. This type of wax can only be used once; it cannot be reliquified so don't let it set inside the icing bag

Bottom left: When the wax has set it will resist colour brushed over the surface. Watercolours, inks, or fabric paints work equally well and when the colours have dried, the wax can be scraped off the paper

Top centre: A white wax crayon is rubbed across a sheet of paper held on top of a piece of decorative cast-iron. The paper is held firmly on the object and the crayon rubbed with an even, firm pressure. The end of a candle can also be used for this process

Bottom centre: After the paper is waxed it is removed from the object and a wash of watercolour, ink or fabric paint is brushed across the surface to show a negative facsimile of the shape and texture of the original object

Top right: The same wax-rubbing technique works with a large assortment of objects and can be used on fabric as well as on paper. Here Noel has used a spiky twig

Bottom right: Noel is painting across the wax texture created by rubbing over a printing block. Patterns borrowed in this way and incorporated into a full scale batik can create almost photographic effects

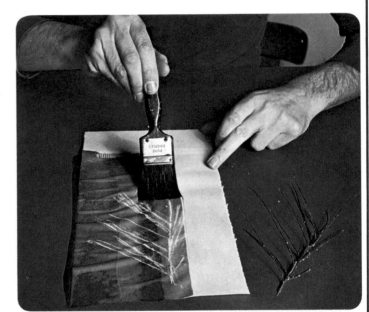

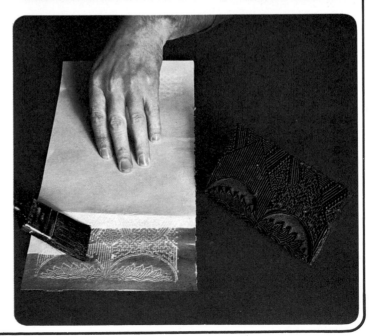

PROJECT 5: EXPERIMENTING WITH WAX

Expand your range of techniques • shaped brushes • three-pronged tjanting • colouring wax with crayons • stencils • starch resist

Batik's traditional instruments are few and simple. Brushes, stamps and pointed sticks were the fairly primitive tools behind the elaborate patterns of Oriental work. The tjanting with multiple spouts was developed to match the Javanese tradition of textures and patterns as detailed as wood grain. During this project Noel demonstrates several techniques that can be used together or separately in your batiks to add different textures and patterns. It is best to gain confidence at first by experimenting.

Tools for parallel marks
You will need: fabric, wax, tjanting with multiple spouts, wide brushes with bristles cut into separate 'fingers'.
What to do: experiment with these tools to draw parallel lines of wax, hatched and chequered effects, converging lines, fan-shaped patterns and other designs.

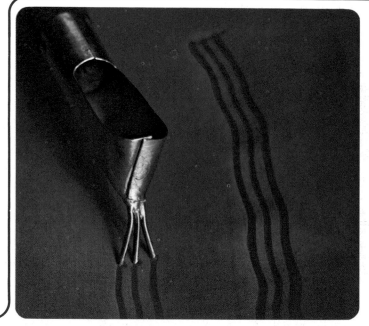

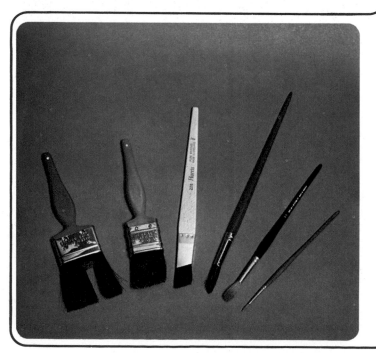

Above: A three-spouted tjanting makes drawing parallel lines a simple task. Other effects such as fan-shaped marks, converging lines and precisely regular dotted and stippled patterns can be created by varying the direction of each stroke

Left: Brushes can be cut like the one on the far left to produce several marks from a single stroke but the range of effects is narrower than with a multiple-spouted tjanting. The bristles tend to spread out if the brush is not used flat

Left: Noel here demonstrates the lines created with a brush cut so that the bristles are divided in two

Below: An assortment of effects created by the three-spouted tjanting and the brush cut in two. Any method of repeating a unit precisely, such as stamps, stencils or these multiple stroke tools can be used to create patterns in batik

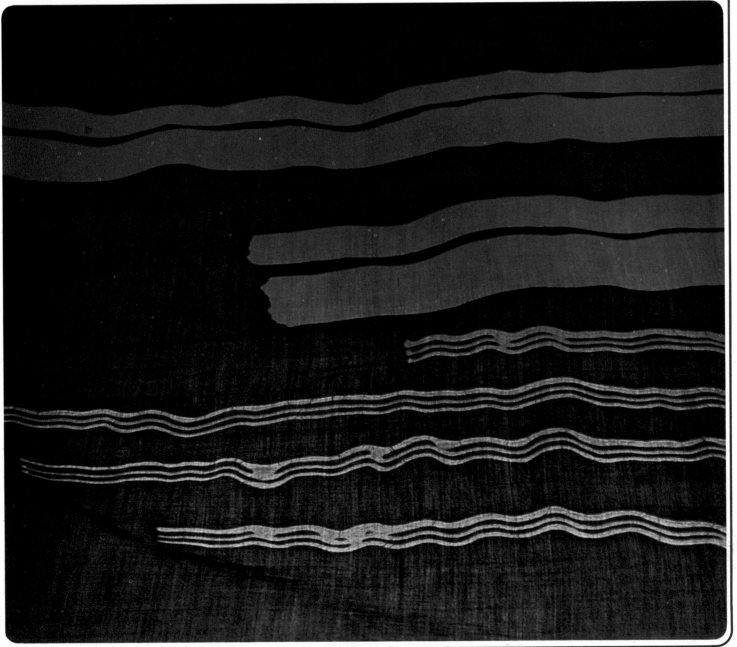

Scratched and scraped effects

You will need: fabric already waxed and dyed—edged and pointed tools: blunt knives, brush-handles etc.
What to do: draw patterns with brush handle, scratching through a layer of wax—experiment with different textures by scraping wax off fabric with the knife blade—redye fabric by immersion to reveal areas where wax has been removed—lift onto newspaper and hang fabric to dry overnight—remove wax from fabric by ironing.

Drawing lines through a layer of wax with any blunt instrument produces an attractive effect when dyed. Noel shows this effect in action by scratching a drawing of a face on a plain geometric shape which he has waxed on previously dyed cloth. The second dye will develop these freely drawn features as it would the normal crackle effect. The mouth was left wax free during the initial waxing.

Coloured wax

You will need: fabric, coloured wax crayons, tjanting, brushes—individual metal pots or a patty tin in a pan of hot water on an electric ring or hotplate to melt the different coloured wax crayons.
What to do: use tjanting and brushes (a different one for each colour of wax) and apply waxes as in the normal batik method—dye the fabric by immersion and hang to dry overnight—remove wax from fabric by ironing between layers of newspaper.

Noel first melts coloured wax crayons in individual metal pots. These different coloured waxes are then applied to the fabric with brush or tjanting in the usual way and the whole fabric is then dyed. The wax resists the action of the dye and when it is ironed out the colour of the wax remains in the fabric. Although the wax crayon colour lacks the intensity of a real dye-colour, this method can achieve varied colour combinations with only one dyeing.

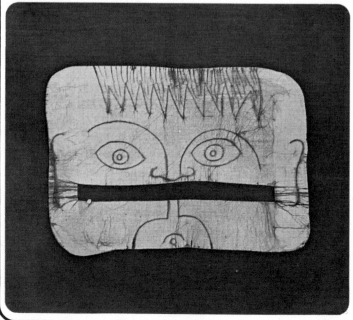

Left: Noel demonstrates how to wax a stretched fabric with different coloured waxes made by melting crayons. This is done simply by putting a piece of crayon into melted wax. These colours can then be mixed together. The wax must be stirred thoroughly to mix the colours well

Below: When the wax has hardened, the fabric is dyed in the normal way by immersion. After the dye has dried, the wax is ironed out of the fabric as usual. Although the iron melts and removes the wax, the colour of the crayons remains in the fabric

Bottom: Here we see the finished batik with the wax ironed out. This method has the advantage of producing several colours with only one dye bath. The same technique can be extended through several waxings and dyeings

Above left: Designs can be incised in layers of wax to create delicate lines with a character that cannot be achieved in any other way. Noel has applied a thick, even layer of wax to a piece of fabric that has already been dyed. Now he is drawing into the wax with a pointed brush-handle. The fabric must be pinned down onto a surface to withstand pressure

Left: This is the finished batik after a second dyeing and with the wax removed. All the features, except the mouth which was left wax-free, were created by scratching through the wax layer so that the second dye could penetrate. Variations of the same technique make use of any instrument that will scrape or scratch a layer of wax such as a knife, the prongs of a fork or the teeth of a comb. Care must be taken not to damage the fabric, of course, but fascinating designs can be produced in this way

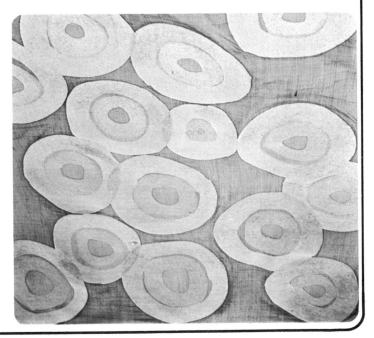

Below: Noel is laying a geometric shape made of transparent plastic onto a piece of dyed fabric. The plastic is adhesive on the underside. Once it is stuck to the fabric he will use it as a stencil and paint molten wax across its edges. The shape of the stencil is added to by a triangle made from strips of adhesive tape. The stencil need not be transparent or adhesive but Noel likes these qualities because he can see the patterns under the stencil while he works and the stencil stays in place. If cardboard is used, it must be held carefully

Right: Noel paints the wax onto the fabric in the space defined between the edge of the stencil and the tape. Careful waxing is essential despite the ready-made edges to prevent too much wax from piling up around the stencil and cracking off when the fabric is handled

Far right: When the waxing is complete the stencil should be removed carefully to avoid peeling wax off the fabric

Below right: The dyed fabric with the pattern defined by the edges of stencil and tape

Project 5: Experimenting with Wax

Stencilling with wax
You will need: fabric, wax, cardboard or stiff paper, cellophane tape, paint brush.
What to do: cut shapes and patterns from the cardboard and fasten them to the fabric with tape—paint wax onto the fabric using the stencil shapes to mask chosen areas—proceed as with normal batik through dyeing and wax removal.

Noel prefers to use transparent material for his stencils, in order to keep an eye on the whole of the fabric while waxing round the stencil. As he often stencils onto stretched fabric, a piece of cardboard would not resist molten wax adequately, since the fabric dips under pressure from the brush. For this reason Noel uses an adhesive material. To place the stencil exactly, Noel registers its position with strips of cellophane tape. This tape can also be used for stencilling – a perfect way to make stripes and straight crisp edges.

How to use paste resist
What you need: fabric, paste resist, dye, thickening agent, paint brush.
What to do: paint the warm paste resist onto the fabric and allow to dry—thicken dye with thickening agent—paint dye onto fabric—remove paste by washing.

Traditional batik employed many kinds of starchy paste resists as alternatives to wax. A good general recipe for such a resist is on page 78. It has to be applied quite thickly with a brush while still hot. The resist should be left for about 24 hours until it is bone-dry. While it is still wet the surface can be decorated by combing, scraping or drawing into it. Although the resist crackles when cold, it is water-soluble, so the dye has to be painted onto the fabric. Thickened dyes are suitable for painting and a recipe to make these dye-paints appears on page 78.

Top: Starch paste can be painted onto paper or fabric to act as a resist. As the paste dries slowly it can be textured by scratching, scraping or combing to allow the dye to penetrate. The paste must be completely dry before any dye-colour is painted on. The dried paste can then be crackled by pulling gently at opposite ends of the cloth to loosen the paste from the fibres

Above: The paste resist with colour painted over it. There are many other such resists that can be used in the same way. Flour and water is the simplest, but pastes can be made using combinations of water with rice flour, laundry starch, bran powder, salt or slaked lime. They can all be applied with a brush or squeezed on with an icing bag

Right: Noel Dyrenforth's *Captive Figure* is boldly patterned and brightly coloured yet it has sinister overtones. The working sequence of dye-colours was yellow, orange, red and finally navy blue

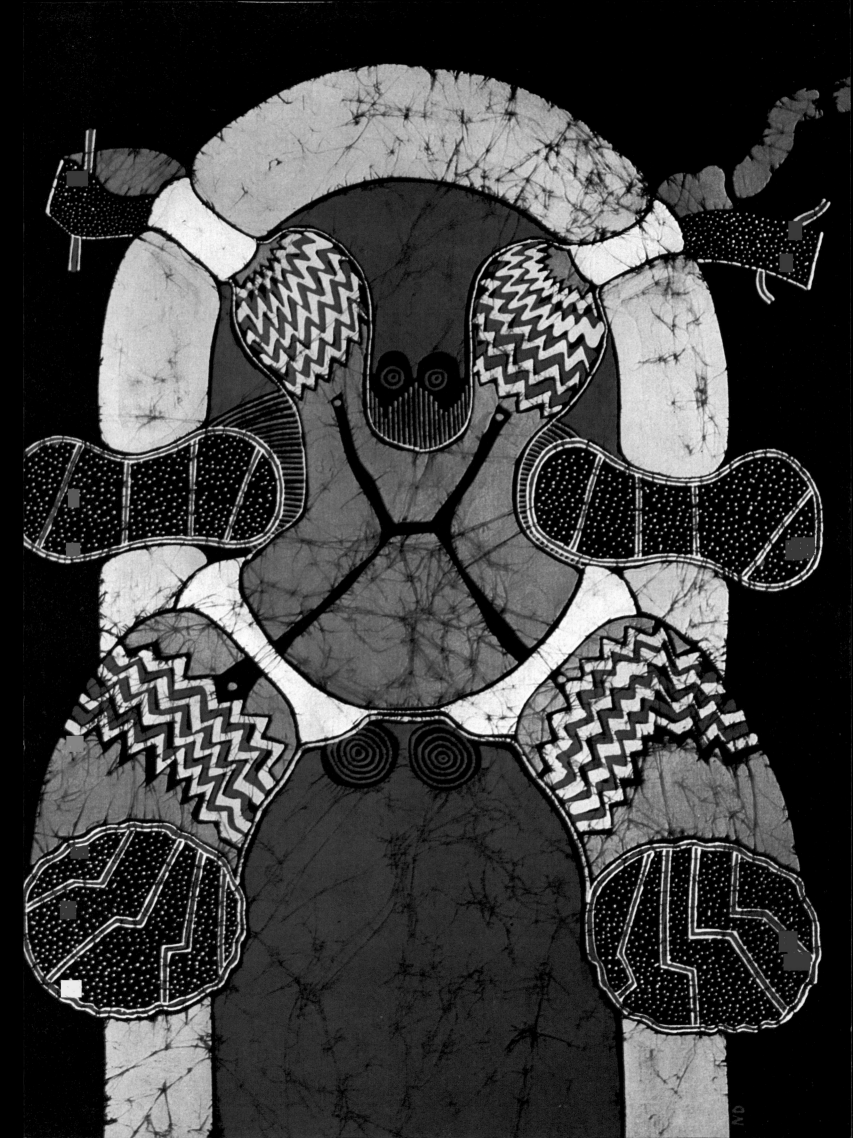

PROJECT 6: A DRESS

**Designing batiks to fit dress patterns •
waxing and dyeing • complete dresses**

You will need: a dress pattern specifying quantity
of fabric to be used—dressmaker's carbon paper—
all the equipment used in Project 1.

What to do: transfer the motifs you have designed
onto the dress pattern—fit the pieces of pattern to
the fabric—use the carbon paper to trace the outlines
of the pattern and the motifs onto the fabric—cut
fabric lengths into rectangles to fit a stretcher—
stretch the fabric—proceed as with normal batik—
after removing the wax, cut pattern shapes out of the
fabric pieces and sew together.

Noel has chosen a loose fitting caftan pattern for this
project. This gives him areas of fabric large enough
to use his design motifs quite freely.

These motifs can be adapted and transferred to
the fabric in either of two ways. The dress pattern
provides shapes for each piece of the garment. The
chosen motifs can be drawn straight onto these
shapes and then both shapes and motifs can be
transferred to the fabric at the same time by using
dressmaker's carbon paper. The second method
simply splits the first into two stages. The pattern
shapes are transferred to the fabric first. The design
motifs are drawn full size onto separate sheets of
tracing paper. These can be moved around underneath
the different parts of the dress pattern to find the
best position. Once this is decided, the motifs can be
traced onto the fabric. The second method takes longer
but seems easier for the beginner who may find it
awkward to visualize the effect of a motif drawn
onto a flimsy dress pattern.

Noel's method of preparing the fabric, waxing and
dyeing it, is exactly the same as for the wall-hanging.
The only difference is that the fabric is too large to
fit one frame so it has been cut into two rectangles
with half the pattern pieces on each one. Naturally
these pieces are not cut out until the end of the batik
process.

The dyeing sequence for this dress is yellow,

Far left, top and bottom: These two working drawings show how the dress pattern Noel has chosen was laid out on two lengths of fabric. This was the most economical positioning for the shapes and for creating lengths of fabric that can be dyed conveniently. The shapes of the pattern pieces and the floral motifs were transferred to the fabric by tracing with dressmaker's carbon paper

Left: Noel is laying a section of the pattern over a full size drawing of the flower motif he intends to use on the sleeves. By moving the pattern around he can ascertain the best placing for the motif

Above: When the dyeing has been completed Noel checks the relationship between the pieces of the pattern and the design motifs. Here he is checking one of the sleeves

Project 6: A Dress

Below, left and right: Both pieces of fabric are shown after the final dyeing. The one on the left is almost wax-free, having been ironed. The one on the right is covered in wax which has been crackled to let the final dye penetrate and create the characteristic marbled effect. All the fabric was dyed in the same dye baths for the same amount of time to make sure that the colours were identical

Right: The complete dress made in sturdy cotton for everyday wear. The fabric was dyed a pale yellow all over before the first waxing. The second colour was orange followed by a dark blue. The fourth and final dye was navy blue which was allowed to crackle through the final waxing which covered almost all of the fabric except the ends of the sleeves. Inset is the sleeve showing the successful integration of the shape of the dress and the colourful batik design

Project 6: A Dress

Right: A dress designed and made by Thea Porter from layers of silk chiffon batik created by Hannah Meckler. The transparency of silk invites the use of startling contrasts. The ribbon-like patterns defined by the dark dye can be seen undulating under several layers of chiffon

Below: Another Thea Porter dress made from a batik on silk chiffon by Hannah Meckler. The silk was dyed with acid dyes, which are especially suited to silk and wool

orange, medium blue, and navy blue which is allowed to crackle through the layer of wax that almost completely covers the rectangles of fabric. As the colours of the various pieces must match precisely, if you cannot dye them together you should prepare your dye baths in exactly the same way: identical ingredients, identical dyeing time. The wax is removed with even more thoroughness than usual, as this fabric will be worn. Noel irons out as much wax as possible and removes the remainder by dry-cleaning. Finally the pattern pieces are cut out of the two fabric lengths and the dress is sewn together, ready to be worn.

The dress design is both unique and practical. The symmetrical placing of the motifs gives the loose fitting caftan a formal air. The sturdy cotton fabric and Procion M dyes guarantee excellent colour fastness — neither light nor washing should fade the dyes — so the dress is perfect for everyday wear.

Batik works equally well with the most flowing styles and the flimsiest of materials. The dresses on these pages were designed by Thea Porter and focus on the glitter and transparency which are the hall-marks of her style. She imports her design materials, bringing carpets, jewels, and glass from North Africa, furniture inlaid with mother-of-pearl from Turkey, and exotic fabrics from India and the Orient to her London dress design and interior-decorating shop. Her design has grown out of diverse traditions, but her choice of fabrics emphasizes the sparkle and flair found in the folk arts of many different countries: Indian fabrics sewn with tiny mirrors, Persian cloths woven with silver thread and embroidered with fringes of glass beads.

The dresses shown here are both made from batiks done on silk chiffon by the South African artist, Hannah Meckler. The streaks and strips of brilliant colour are produced by Sennelier dyes. These French dyes are slightly luminous and specially blended for use on silk.

BATIK TODAY

Modern artists working
with batik • variations of technique •
different styles and ideas

The possibilities of batik are being exploited by increasing numbers of artists and designers. In this section we look at the work and methods of several artists, all of whom demonstrate the versatility of batik as a medium.

Batik's practical tradition — producing decorative but everyday clothes — is still alive and well in the United States. Charlotte Freeman produces a wide range of functional fabrics for shops and clients in New York and London: cotton caftans, silk scarves, capes and shawls, velvet dresses and cushions. The silk chiffon shawl illustrated on this page is pure batik. The design, a Jazz-Age dancer, is drawn in lively lines and dots applied with a tjanting. These waxed lines form the guide for washes of dye-colour freely painted onto both layers of the gauzy shawl. Many of her other garments use the tie and dye technique to give a dappled basis of pattern and colour on which she then draws with wax, the final dyes being painted directly onto the fabric.

Thetis Blacker has travelled widely in southern Asia and has worked at the Javanese Batik Research Institute, refining and intensifying her techniques for dyeing fabrics. Her concern is to communicate each image in her work with the greatest possible power and precision. For her, much of this power comes from the colour vibrations which she creates with twelve or more dyeings and bleachings of each batik.

Norma Straszakowna is a young Scotswoman who works only on silk. Her batiks are always square and usually tiny, twelve or sixteen inches, as in the works shown here. She often paints directly onto wet silk, using pale tones at first, but always increasing each colour's richness as she works. She also uses a toothbrush, flicking its dye-soaked bristles with her finger to spray a speckle of colour onto the fabric.

Few modern artists exploit the crisp precision emphasized by Oriental batik. Sylvia Nestor Robinson pays homage to Oriental style as well as technique in her three-fold lacquer-framed screen. The areas

Top left: The vibrant colour of *Phoenix and Fish* by Thetis Blacker is the result of a dozen applications of dye, some added by dipping and some by painting. The entire surface of the fabric is split into tiny mosaic units with luminous colour shining through the borders. The artist's technique is more like that of a painter in that there is no regular sequence of waxing and dyeing. Areas of colour are added or bleached out at every stage of the batik

Centre left: Charlotte Freeman painted acid dyes directly onto wax outlines made with a tjanting to produce this fringed shawl. The fabric is silk chiffon, double-layered so that the design will not be affected if the shawl is worn over a patterned dress. When used for batik, acid dyes must be used cool. Although this reduces the maximum brilliance of the dye, most artists who make silk batiks still prefer to use acid dyes

Above: *Grass Song* is a batik by Norma Starszakowna. A very fine brush was used to paint the two tiny faces which are the focal point of the design. The diamond shape framing the two heads is delicately spotted and dappled with colour. Some of the dark spots were spattered on with a dye-soaked brush. The dappled effect was produced by the bleaching action of soap powder sprinkled onto the wet silk. The surface was then covered with absorbent paper and ironed dry

Bottom left: *Dream Stone* is another batik by Norma Starszakowna. This artist always works on silk and usually on a very small scale. Her technique mixes direct painting and immersion dyeing. The first colours are often painted onto wet fabric using several colours at once and letting them merge and dissolve into each other. The fabric is only immersed in two or three dye-colours

of colour are very sharply defined, with the different textures, bark, earth, feathers, and leaves, suggested by patches of colour like a mosaic.

Michael O'Connell lives and works in the country-side just beyond London's northern fringe. He enjoys working with paste resists on thick fabrics which have a pronounced texture. Thick tapioca paste was a traditional resist for coarsely woven African cloths, as was mud. Michael devised his own resist for very large batiks, based on china clay. His largest work measures fifty yards long and five yards high, and even though it was divided into seven sections he had to hire a dance hall as a studio. The resist was finally removed with a powerful hose and a stiff broom! He combines starch resist and wax on the same batik, as in the illustration on page 71. Paste was used first to define the thick red line which acts as an outline for the colours to follow. The paste simply forms a surface crust on the fabric and though it resists dye which is painted on, it can be scraped and washed off the fabric much more easily than wax. Once the paste was completely removed the subsequent dyes were resisted by wax.

Deryck Henley, self-taught as a portrait-painter, turned away from oil-paint, attracted by batik's natural materials. His design here is based on a pencil drawing, taken from life, and recomposed on the fabric. One of the main problems is to control the build-up of tones in order to create a convincing face. He deals with this by using a lot of very pale dyes. Variety of tone within a single coloured area can be controlled by direct painting, but he has also evolved

Below: Batik by Dr Amri Yahya, who lives and works in Java. The colourless background of the batik has been completely covered with beeswax. Although most of the colours have been painted directly onto the fabric, the blue and green areas were dyed by immersion. The gauzy areas of crackle are the result of using paraffin wax. The tjanting's calligraphic marks produce feathery rippling textures in the painted sections

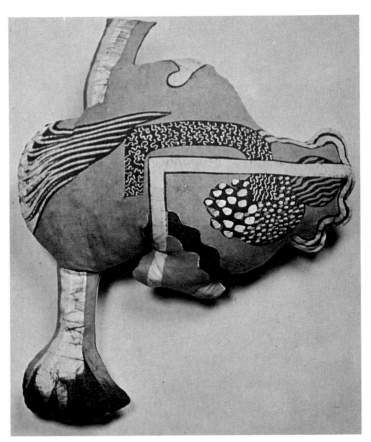

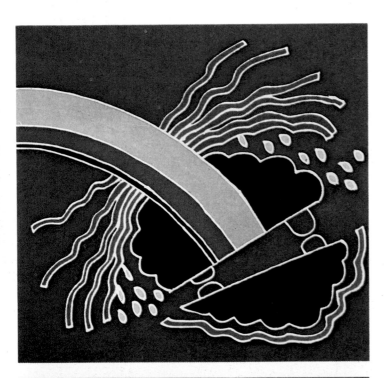

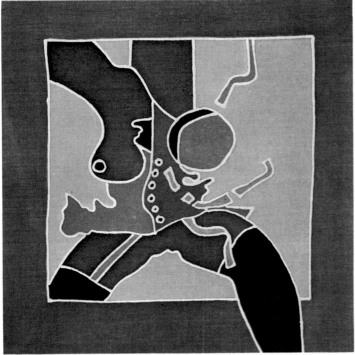

Above left: For this batik Noel Dyrenforth used the method of painting different coloured dyes into a pattern outlined in wax as in project 2. The crispness of the resulting batik is produced by the even width of the outline

Left: A further example of this direct-painting technique in a very similar composition. On this batik the outlines have faded into the background. As every shape is different from the next it is the areas of solid colour that are the most important element

Above: This batik by Noel Dyrenforth is in a class of its own, somewhere between a cushion and a sculpture. It was cleaned and then cut up, stuffed with foam rubber, and sewn together

Right: *Aztec Rainbow* by Noel Dyrenforth compresses a wealth of pattern and texture into a clearly organized and satisfying design. The first waxing covered the curved patterns in the small right-angled triangles. The first dye was pale yellow and while the fabric was still wet the bottom edge was dipped in pale blue so that this dye crept up the yellow fabric. The next waxing covered areas of yellow and outlined the rainbow. The rainbow colours were then painted in and completely covered by wax. The next dye, a deep turquoise, was painted across the top two-thirds of the fabric. This mixed with the yellow to produce a greyish-blue which was partly covered in the next waxing. An olive-green dye was painted on to define the largest triangle and finally the wax on the bottom third of the fabric was crackled and a navy blue dye brushed over all the exposed areas

Above: Another batik from Noel Dyrenforth's typewriter series. In this series Noel has examined several views of this machine, bringing out different textures and ideas

a dyeing method which he feels is more in sympathy with the nature of batik and often gives better results. He floats the fabric, face up, on top of the dye bath. The colour soaks through very slowly and just unevenly enough to lend a subtle variety to the flat colour.

Juliet Bloye describes her technique as letting batik do half the work. The other half comes from the picture — usually a landscape — which she tries to recreate as mood and pattern. *The Memory Garden* takes its title from a gravestone, but the landscape is a real one. This batik is built from six different dyeings: turquoise, pink, lemon, chrome-yellow, blue and a final brown which veins through the carefully crackled wax. This brown is not produced as a dye, but by fast colour salts (recipe on page 78) which give the previous dyes that are still exposed the earthy hue of traditional Javanese dyes. This only works with Procion M fibre-reactive dyes.

There is a healthy modern tradition of Javanese batik which blends that island's technical heritage with influence drawn from European painting. Dr. Amri Yahya is a Professor at the Academy of Fine Arts in Djakarta. At first sight his batiks resemble a modern abstract painting: elegantly composed marks with no subject other than line and colour. In fact the designs have as their subject the varied techniques used in batik itself.

If Noel Dyrenforth's batiks have a single factor in common it is activity. Although each work has a formal grandeur, the result of clearly defined and symmetrically arranged blocks of colour, this symmetry is almost always upset in an unexpected way. Inside each block of colour there is more activity: one texture fading into another, or an almost imperceptible gradation of colour obtained by dipping the edge of the wet fabric in a dye bath. The batiks by Noel which are illustrated here conspire to make the technique seem effortless, but they demonstrate his mastery of batik as an expressive medium.

APPENDICES

Recipes for dyes • suppliers of batik
equipment • further reading

Recipes

The most suitable dyes for batik on the recommended
fabrics are cold water dyes. These are Dylon and
Procion M. Instructions for using Dylon and Procion
dyes are given below. Other dyes are sold with
manufacturer's instructions which should be followed
exactly. Don't forget to wear rubber gloves while
dyeing and handling wet fabric.

Dylon cold water dyes

25 colours in smallest 6 g (gramme) tins, 12 colours in
30 g tins. The larger colour range can be bought direct
from Dylon in 500 g packages.
Method, using 6 g tin:
1 Pierce tin and dissolve contents in 20 fl. oz.
   (0·57 litres) warm water. Stir well and pour into
   bowl.
2 For each tin of dye, dissolve 4 tablespoons salt
   and 1 envelope Dylon Cold Fix (or 1 heaped
   tablespoon washing soda) in hot water. Stir well
   and add to dye.
3 Top up with the minimum quantity of hot water
   sufficient to cover the batik to be dyed.

Procion M dyes

These include Dylon, Fabdec, Fibrec and Putnam
assorted colours in $\frac{1}{2}$ oz. to 1 lb. (15 g to 454 g)
containers. They are clear and brilliant in colour,
simple to use, intermixable and exceedingly fast,
resisting both light and washing. They are fibre-
reactive dyes, fixed on the fabric by direct chemical
linkage, and so need no heating or boiling.
The method below will dye 2–3 square yards or
metres of material; multiply or divide the quantities for
other sizes:
1 Make a paste of 1–3 teaspoons dye in a little cold
   water. Add 10 fl. oz. (0·28 l) warm water.
2 Dissolve, *separately*, 2 level tablespoons urea in
   20 fl. oz. (0·57 l) lukewarm water.

Lonely Embraces by Noel Dyrenforth uses the same technique
as *Aztec Rainbow*. The central Y-shape that dominates the
design is softened by a series of luminous colours that seem
to melt into each other. This effect began with the whole fabric
being dyed a pale pink. While still wet the lower edge of the
fabric was dipped into a pale brown dye and then almost
immediately dipped into pale blue. These colours were made
by adding dye to the first dye bath of pale pink. When these
colours were dry, the Y-shape was completely waxed. From
then on each new dye produced different colour mixes in each
half of the fabric. The dyeing sequence proceeded from brilliant
orange to a cool brown, then dark green and finally navy blue

3 Mix 1 and 2 together in bowl large enough to hold fabric.

4 Dissolve 4 level tablespoons salt in 20 fl. oz. (0·57 l) hot water. Add to dye solution.

5 Wet the fabric. Immerse it in the dye solution for 5 minutes. Keep the fabric submerged, and keep it moving continuously. Add more water if needed.

6 A previously prepared alkaline solution: 1 tablespoon washing soda dissolved in a little warm water. Remove fabric from dye bath. Stir in this solution. NB: the dye bath will only remain stable for 2–3 hours after soda is added.

7 Replace fabric in dye bath for 15 to 45 minutes, depending on strength of colour required. Stir occasionally.

8 Remove fabric and hang to dry. Fixation begins immediately.

9 After final dyeing, colour will fix best in a warm humid atmosphere; then rinse out excess dye.

Household dyes (hot water dyes)

These are all-purpose dyes and are readily available. They can be used on cottons, silks, linen, wool and many synthetic fibres. They are sold under such brand names as Dylon, Multipurpose, RIT, Tintex and Putnams. Although designed as hot water dyes, they can be adapted to a cold water method and can therefore be used for batik. Household dyes are not as colour fast as cold water dyes, however, and should be used only if cold water dyes are not available. For the cold water dyeing necessary for batik, you should add double the amount of household dye as is specified in recipes for cold water dyes. Mix the dye to a paste with a little hot water and then proceed as though dyeing with cold water dyes — as described in the recipe above.

Direct painting with dye

Procion M dyes can be mixed to a suitable consistency for painting onto a fabric in conjunction with wax or paste resist. Direct painting is often an easier way to colour a small area of fabric than immersing the whole batik in a dye bath. There are several commercial thickening agents which give the dye a paintable consistency, such as Manutex RS, Halltex and Keltex.

Thickening dyes for direct application:

1 Mix 1 teaspoon Calgon (water softener) in 20 fl. oz. (0·57 l) cold water.

2 Dissolve 10 tablespoons urea in 10 fl. oz. (0·28 l) warm water.

3 Mix 1 and 2 together.

4 Add 2 teaspoons thickening agent slowly, stirring to an even consistency. After standing for at least 30 minutes, but preferably overnight, this mixture will become a smooth clear gum ready for use.

5 Mix the dye powder to a paste with a little cold water. NB: 5 level teaspoons of Procion M dye will give dark shades; 3 teaspoons give medium shades; 1 teaspoon a pale shade.

6 Before painting: add 1½ teaspoons bicarbonate of soda and 1 teaspoon washing soda. NB: the dye bath will remain stable for only 2–3 hours after soda is added, therefore proportion the soda to the quantity of dye you propose to use immediately.

7 After using this method dry the fabric in a warm humid place for 24–48 hours.

Brentamines

These can only be used with Procion M reactive dyes. The earthy brown colours characteristic of many Javanese batiks can be produced by this method. After the final dyeing the cloth is dipped into a solution of Brentamine Fast Black K Salt.

1 Dissolve 1 teaspoon K salt in 20 fl. oz. (0·57 l) warm water, add 1½ tablespoons salt and stir. Allow to cool.

2 Immerse the dry fabric for 5–10 minutes.

3 Rinse and then boil the fabric to remove excess dye.

Paste resist

For use on either fabric or paper to resist direct painting with dye. As the consistency depends on the effect you want to achieve, the proportion of each ingredient given here is simply a guide. The simplest effective recipe is just to mix white flour with water. All these pastes when dry can be crumbled off cloth and paper. The fabric will probably need a final rinse in warm water.

1 Mix 1 tablespoon rice flour, 1 tablespoon white flour, and ½ tablespoon powdered laundry starch in a little cold water. Remove all lumps.

2 Add the mixture to 15 fl. oz. (0·42 l) water and heat in a double boiler for about 10 minutes.

3 Apply the paste hot.

Discharge dyeing

This is simply a method for removing colour by bleaching. Dylon, Tintex, Rit, and Putnam all produce colour removers. After wax resist has been applied to the dyed fabric this is immersed in a weak solution of bleach for a short period.

1 Strong bleach solution is 1 part bleach to 3 parts water; the normal solution is 1 part bleach to 5 parts water.

2 Immerse fabric. Length of time depends on bleaching effect desired. But keep checking the effect. If left too long, the bleach will eat into the fabric.

3 Remove fabric and immediately rinse thoroughly.

4 Dry fabric and remove wax.

NB: this technique is not recommended for use on silk.

Fabrics

Fabrics made with natural fibres include mercerized and unmercerized cotton, muslin, cotton velveteen, corduroy, batiste, percale, duck, canvas, pure linen and fine wool. Heavily textured or open-weave fabrics present difficulties when waxing. A small amount of water softener, such as Calgon, will help fabric to receive dye evenly.

Papers

These should be tough as they will have to stand up to paste, wax, inks, watercolour and poster paint. Hot press watercolour paper is suitably strong, interestingly textured, but fairly expensive. Many art supply stores stock Oriental papers which are strong and marvellously varied in tone and texture. Even so you must work quickly and with soft brushes or the paper can turn to mush.

Suppliers

United Kingdom
Candle Makers Suppliers
4 Beaconsfield Terrace Road, London, W14.
This company has comprehensive mail-order and can provide a variety of waxes including granulated batik wax, paraffin wax, beeswax and cold wax; dyes including Procion M, Brentamine Fast Black K Salt and Sennelier silk dyes; hog-bristle brushes, tjantings in three sizes including multiple-spouted varieties, frames, thermometers and chemicals.

Crafts Unlimited
178 Kensington High Street, London W8.
Mail-order: P.O. Box 48, Enfield, Middlesex.
Deka dyes in 32 colours, batik wax and tools, wax crayons, waterproof inks, fabric inks.

Dryad Handicrafts
Northgates, Leicester.
Wax, brushes, tjantings, silk and cotton fabrics.

Dylon International Ltd.
Worsley Bridge Road, London SE26.
Dylon cold water dyes (these are also available from most hardware stores), Procion M reactive dyes, Manutex RS and other chemicals. Dylon have a consumer advice bureau at the above address to answer any written queries about dyeing.

Hobby Horse Ltd.
17 Langton Street, London SW10.
Wax, tjantings, frames, dyes including Procion M, Dylon, and Sennelier silk dyes.

Pongees Ltd.
Empire house, St. Martins-le-Grand, London EC1
Silks.

Winsor and Newton Ltd.
Wealdstone, Harrow, Middlesex.
Printex fabric printing colours.

North America
Many local art and craft suppliers carry batik equipment. Specific dyes and distributors are listed below.

Aiko's Art Materials
714 North Wabash Avenue, Chicago, Ill. 60611.
Dyes and tools; Japanese art supplies.

Carousel Crafts Inc.
6401 Westline, Houston, Texas 77036.
Dylon cold water and fiber-reactive dyes.

Craft Community
Box C, El Cernito, Calif. 94530.
Wax, unsized cotton, brushes, fiber-reactive dyes.

Dick Blick Art Materials
P.O. Box 1267, Galesburg, Ill. 61401.
Dick Blick dyes, Putnam dyes, wax, tjantings, batik frames, pigments.

Dylawn Products Co.
95 218th Street, Queens Village, N.Y. 11429.
Fiber-reactive dyes.

Earth Guild
149 Putnam Avenue, Cambridge, Mass. 02139.
Dyes, frames, wax, brushes, tjantings, Keltex.

Fibrec
2795 16th Street, San Francisco, Calif. 94103.
Fiber-reactive dyes, thickeners, waxes, tjantings.

Putnam Dyes
Quincy, Ill. 62301.
All-purpose dyes, fiber-reactive dyes.

Rit
Best Foods Division CPC International, 1137 W. Morris Street, Indianapolis, Ind. 46206.
Rit all-purpose and liquid dyes.

Sax Arts and Crafts
316 N. Milwaukee, Milwaukee, Wis. 53202.
Batik supplies and dyes.

Stein Hall and Co.
285 Madison Avenue, New York, N.Y. 10017.
Halltex (sodium alginate).

Craft Publications

The following can be recommended:
Craft Horizons published bi-monthly by the American Crafts Council, 44 West 53rd Street, New York, N.Y.
Crafts published bi-monthly by the Crafts Advisory Committee, 12 Waterloo Place, London, SW1.
Creative Crafts published monthly by Pitmans Periodicals Ltd., 41 Parker Street, London, WC2.

Craft Galleries

The American Crafts Council at the address given above is the only national membership, multi-media organization. It can put enquirers in touch with the many specialist societies, summer schools, and college courses in the crafts. It also maintains the Museum of Contemporary Crafts, at 29 West 53rd Street, New York.

In England the Crafts Advisory Committee is a Government financed non-membership organization which assists craftsmen and informs the public from its own gallery in Waterloo Place (see above).

The British Crafts Centre is a membership society with a gallery at 43 Earlham Street, Covent Garden, London, WC2. It also sells members' work from its gallery inside the Victoria and Albert Museum in South Kensington, London, SW7. The Victoria and Albert is the national museum of decorative art and has regular exhibitions of historic and modern crafts.

Craft Societies

Each of the English-speaking countries has a wide range of specialist societies. Their membership is usually a mix of amateur and professional craftsmen plus non-craftsmen supporters, all drawn from a conveniently sized area. Contact with local groups can usually be made through a national body.

U.S.A. and U.K.: See Craft Publications on page 79.

Canada: Canadian Guild of Crafts, 2025 Peel Street, Montreal, Quebec.

Canadian Craftsmen's Association, P.O. Box 2431, Station 'D', Ottawa.

Australia: The Crafts Council of Australia, 27 King Street, Sydney, New South Wales.

Further Reading

Belfer, Nancy, *Designing in Batik and Tie Dye*, Davis Publications Inc., New York 1972; London 1973.

Gibbs, Joanifer, *Batik Unlimited*, Watson-Guptill Publications, New York 1974; Pitman Publishing, London 1974.

Jameson, Norma, *Batik for Beginners*, Studio Vista, London 1970.

Krevitsky, Nik, *Batik: Art and Craft*, Van Nostrand Reinhold, New York 1973; London 1964.

Meilach, Dona Z., *Contemporary Batik and Tie-Dye*, Crown Publishers Inc., New York 1972; George Allen and Unwin Ltd., London 1973.

Nea, Sara, *Batik: Material, Techniques, Design*, Van Nostrand Reinhold, New York 1972; London 1971.

Robinson, Stuart, *History of Dyed Textiles*, Studio Vista, London 1969; M.I.T. Press, Cambridge, Mass. 1970.

Robinson, Stuart and Robinson, Patricia, *Exploring Fabric Printing*, Mills and Boon, London 1970; Branford, Newton Centre, Mass. 1972.

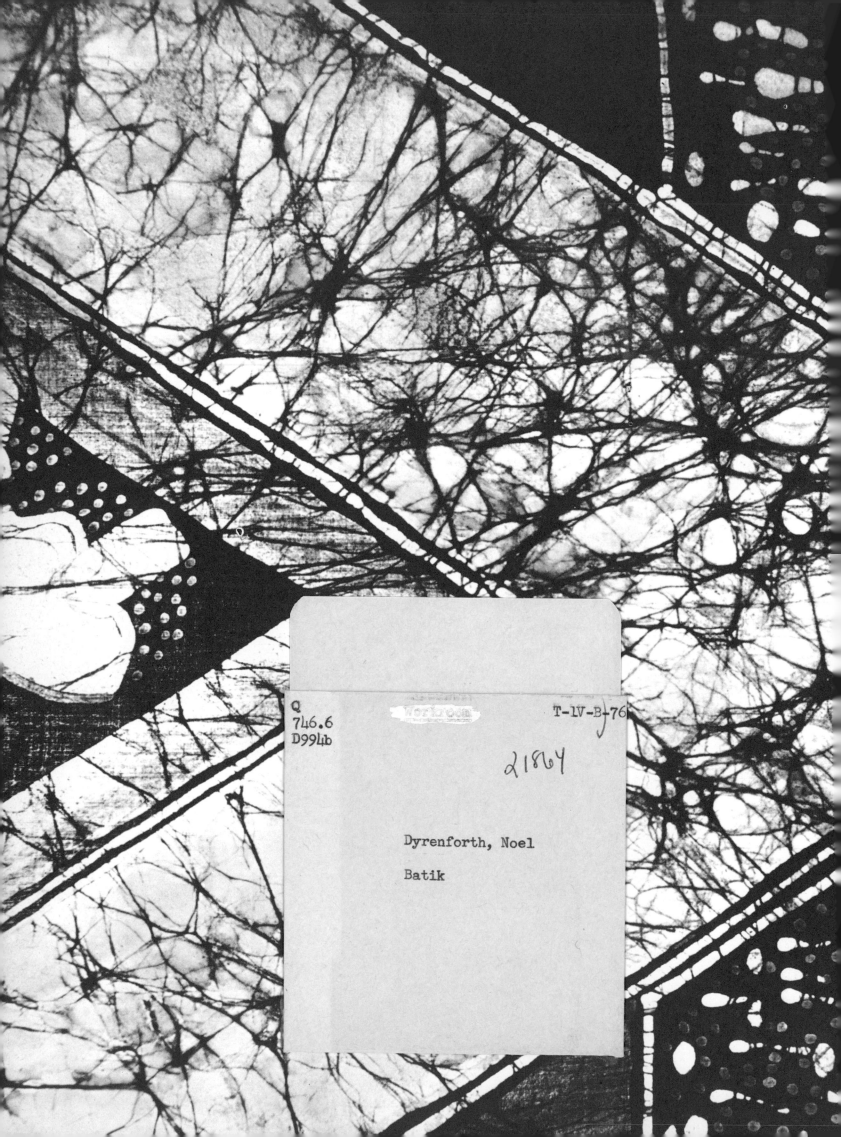